GOD'S WORD
ABOUT SEX

AND RELATED TOPICS

*The Bible's Message
from Creation through the Return from Babylon*

MARY KUHLMANN ANTHOLZ

ELECTRIC
MOON
PUBLISHING

Copyright 2020 by Mary Kuhlmann Antholz

Published by Electric Moon Publishing, LLC

©2020 *God's Word about Sex and Related Topics: The Bible's Message from Creation through the Return from Babylon* / Mary Kuhlmann Antholz

Paperback ISBN-13: 978-1-943027-47-7
E-book ISBN-13: 978-1-943027-48-4

Electric Moon Publishing, LLC
P.O. Box 466
Stromsburg, NE 68666
info@emoonpublishing.com

All rights reserved. No part of this publication may be reproduced, distributed, or transmitted in any form or by any means, including photocopying, recording, or other electronic or mechanical methods, without the prior written permission of the publisher, except in the case of brief quotations embodied in critical reviews and certain other noncommercial uses permitted by copyright law. For permission requests, write to the publisher.

The opinions and quotations of the author are not necessarily that of the publisher or its affiliates/contractors/printers. Author retains all intellectual property rights. Contact author for questions or disputes.

Unless otherwise indicated, Scripture quotations are from the ESV˚ Bible (*The Holy Bible, English Standard Version˚*), copyright © 2001 by Crossway, a publishing ministry of Good News Publishers. All rights reserved.

Scripture taken from *The Holy Bible, An American Translation* by William F. Beck, Leader Publishing Company, New Haven, Missouri, 1976 edition. Copyright 2020 © William F. Beck Estates. Used by permission of the publisher, Lutheran News, Inc. Wherever this is the source of a Biblical quotation, it is identified as "Beck."

Scripture taken from the Holy Bible, NEW INTERNATIONAL VERSION®, NIV® / NEW INTERNATIONAL READER'S VERSION ® NIrV ® Copyright © 1973, 1978, 1984, 2011 by Biblica, Inc.® Used by permission. All rights reserved worldwide.

Scripture taken from the New International Reader's Version (NIrV). Copyright © 1996, 1998 by Biblica.

Scriptures marked KJV are taken from the KING JAMES VERSION (KJV): KING JAMES VERSION, public domain.

Cover and Interior Design by Lyn Rayn / Electric Moon Publishing Creative Services
Author photo courtesy of Michelle Kristine Photography. Cover photo by iStock.

Printed in the United States of America

www.emoonpublishing.com

CONTENTS

FOREWORD

HOLY SCRIPTURE HAS a lot to say about sex. It tells us what God's intent was for sex. It also has a lot to say about the way sin has corrupted sex from the original divine plan. God's intention was that sex would be part of the "*very good*" of the original creation and the world without sin. In fact, sex is included in the original command to Adam and Eve and all their descendants to "*be fruitful and multiply*."

But when sin entered the world, the good thing God created was corrupted and made into something it was never intended to be. That's where we are today. That's the world we live in. The struggle for Christians is to avoid a knee-jerk reaction, on one hand, and think of sex as something wrong or as a guilty pleasure; or, on the other hand, adopt the world's view of sex as something that is "all about me," meaning it must serve the individual's pleasure.

When we look at sex in its original biblical context, we see the great gift God intended it to be. We see love and union—the looking out for and placing the good of the other person first—and the growth of the love and union, resulting, usually, in children.

This is the true benefit of *God's Word about Sex*. It is a valuable commentary on all passages in Scripture that talk about sex. Far from being a dry textbook, the author addresses many key theological points in a manner that is easy to understand. Because of the nature of this book, the reader will get a fine overview of the topic. From there, if desired, he or she can further investigate those passages that whet the appetite, which leads to being equipped by God's Word to stand against the current trends of society. The reader will be able, as a result of reading this book, to explain in an accurate but gentle way the teaching of Scripture to those who are opposed to it or question it because of what the society is saying.

This book is an excellent read and study and a springboard to further discovery, reflection, and conversation.

God bless your reading of *God's Word about Sex.*

—**Pastor Gerhard Grabenhofer,** parish pastor
Translator of *God Grant It: Daily Devotions from C. F. W. Walther*
Participant translator of *Exodus of the Eight Hundred,* award recipient from
Concordia Historical Institute in their Major Publication category.

INTRODUCTION

CHRISTIANS ARE OFTEN accused of cherry-picking—spouting proof texts in support of our favorite theories while totally ignoring passages that may give a different view. Our detractors make a valid point. By only supplying our children and grandchildren with verses that deal with the problems we faced at their age or the ones with which we think they are currently contending, we fail to give them the answers they will need in the culture they will be living in ten years from now.

Instead, perhaps it's time for all of us to take a good look at everything the Bible says about sex. Only then will we be able to sort out God's opinions from human viewpoints and leave a complete legacy of truth for future generations.

Sex was part of the *very good* world that existed at the end of earth's first week (**Genesis 1:31**). But Satan has gone out of his way to make a mess of what was perfect when God created it. He's constantly working to pervert our perception of sex—in many ways, turning it into one of the most polluted subjects on our planet. Because the devil has so abused this gift, God's Word is filled with warnings to avoid those corruptions, including many examples of people who have tried to compromise God's original intentions for sex.

In studying the problems humans have encountered as they tried to add their own twists to God's perfect plan for sex, we find a lot of people who have struggles in this area. We also discover that God has an infinite amount of patience with individuals and nations, constantly forgiving those who repent of their errors and return to Him and His ways.

But when a nation—any nation—tips the scales too far in the direction of wrong—when perversion becomes a way of life—then God will eventually remove His hand of protection from that country, no matter how faithful their ancestors were, and He'll allow foreign nations and natural disasters to destroy them. Thus, God's view of sex is an important topic both for personal and cultural reasons.

We worry about land, water, and air pollution. Should we not also be concerned about the sexual pollution we see all around us? God says some things are good and some are bad. And yet, we so often choose to try the bad, never considering whether the designer of our minds and bodies could have our best interests at heart. We refuse to think He might even know what He's talking about.

We do so because we're human. So were Abraham, Jacob, David, Solomon, and billions of others. I strongly suspect God gives us those biblical accounts as a warning, so we can view their problems from a distance and not walk in their paths.

We can't clean up the whole world. We can, however, start spring cleaning in our own lives. Let's begin by finding out for sure what God says is good—and what He says is bad—and then we'll know how to sort the actions and attitudes we find within ourselves.

Knowing that some of the great heroes of the Bible also had feet of clay, perhaps we will be equipped to reach out to others with the light at the end of the tunnel—forgiveness and new life in Christ.

As stated in the copyrights, unless otherwise indicated, Scripture quotations are from the ESV˙ Bible (*The Holy Bible, English Standard Version*˙), copyright © 2001 by Crossway, a publishing ministry of Good News Publishers. All rights reserved.

All quotations in chapters two and six, as well as scattered verses elsewhere, are from *The Holy Bible, An American Translation* by William F. Beck, Leader Publishing Company, New Haven, Missouri, 1976 edition. Copyright 2020 © William F. Beck Estates. Used by permission of the publisher, Lutheran News, Inc. Wherever this is the source of a Biblical quotation, it is identified as "Beck."

Verses of Scripture are in italics. My comments are in normal type. I shall attempt to include all verses that deal with this subject, from any angle, usually in the order in which they appear in the text.

To avoid giving birth to a set of encyclopedias, however, I have summarized longer sections of Scripture in some cases, rather than quoting them in their entirety. In other cases, for the same reason, I have only quoted portions of verses. Therefore, I urge you to read this book with your Bible close at hand, so you may compare my statements with those entire portions of Scripture.

Most importantly, take God's Word as truth. Take my words as comments.

I've been reading the Bible daily, cover to cover, for fifty-eight of my seventy-five years. I've been single, married, divorced, a single parent, and now a grandmother. I'm an avid reader and an eager observer of God at work in this world.

Among the sources I have studied are many books and magazines often called "creation literature." Those have included, among others, publications and presentations of both Bible-Science Association and Institute for Creation Research. Although I cannot cite chapter and verse, some of my better observations had their beginnings in those sources.

While I do have many comments on this subject, I lay no claim to be an expert. I'm not the authority. God is! God is the One who created the structures, the hormones, the nerve endings–and yes, even those feelings of romantic love the Greeks called *eros*—all of which combine to make possible His gift we call *sex*.

1

FROM THE BEGINNING

WELCOME TO AN exploration of *God's Word about Sex*. You're going to meet characters you never heard about in Sunday school. Most of you will discover passages you wouldn't expect to see in Scripture. And you'll learn that many of the familiar Bible heroes had problems with sex. After all, just like us, they were human.

Human sexuality is a topic that is very important to God—so important that He speaks of the marriage relationship as a mirror and example of the connection He wants with all who believe in Him. I suspect that's why He created our bodies with the capacity to enjoy what might otherwise have been simply the action necessary to bring forth a new generation.

Therefore, we'll have the biblical discussion of sex on two levels.

The most obvious one speaks to the intimate physical relationship between two human beings. A study of these passages will help us understand the attitude God expects us to have toward our bodies and those of the people whose paths we cross.

More subtly, we'll examine the parallel relationship between God and His people. Scattered through both the Old and New Testaments are statements pointing to God as a husband or bridegroom. The descendants of Abraham as a nation—then later the believers in Jesus as the Messiah—are characterized either as His bride or His unfaithful wife.

Second Timothy 3:16 tells us, *All Scripture is breathed out by God and* *profitable for teaching, for reproof, for correction, and for training in righteousness.* So in this book and its companion volume, let's look at all the Bible verses dealing with sex, start to finish, to get a picture of God's view on this subject. That, in turn, should help clear up some of the confusion prevalent in our world, even among Christians.

ADAM AND EVE

Genesis 1:27–28. *So God created man in his own image, in the image of God he created him; male and female he created them. And God blessed them. And God said to them, "Be fruitful and multiply and fill the earth and subdue it."*

That seems pretty straightforward. This declaration comes from the creation narrative as written directly by God Himself (perhaps on tablets of stone?).

Genesis 1:31. *And God saw everything that he had made, and behold, it was very good.*

That included people with the ability to have children.

Genesis 2:18–22. The creation story was also recorded in the portion of Adam's *toledoth* Moses used when compiling Genesis. It, therefore, has more details about the history of human origins. To catch the pertinent highlights:

Then the LORD God said, "It is not good that the man should be alone; I will make him a helper fit for him" . . . But for Adam there was not found a helper fit for him [from among the animals]. *So the LORD God caused a deep sleep to fall upon the man, and while he slept took one of his ribs and closed up its place with flesh. And the rib that the LORD God had taken from the man he made into a woman and brought her to the man.*

As with the creation of Adam, God didn't just speak Eve into existence. Her body, too, was carefully crafted, in part, by removing the Y chromosomes from Adam's donor tissue and doubling the X's.

Genesis 2:23–24. *Then the man said, "This at last is bone of my bones and flesh of my flesh; she shall be called Woman, because she was taken out of Man." Therefore, a man shall leave his father and his mother and hold fast to his wife, and they shall become one flesh.*

These words were even quoted by Jesus, as recorded in **Matthew 19** and **Mark 10**. In any case, this was the declaration by Adam of the definition of marriage.

Genesis 2:25. *And the man and his wife were both naked and were not ashamed.*

Even in heaven, it seems we'll be wearing clothes (robes, see **Revelation 7:14**), but that wasn't the original intention.

Everything was fantastic in the garden until the devil tricked Eve, she persuaded Adam, and they did the one thing God told them not to do.

Genesis 3:7. *Then the eyes of both were opened, and they knew that they were naked. And they sewed fig leaves together and made themselves loincloths.*

What a contrast! It almost makes you wonder if the devil targeted that part of our human nature intentionally.

Genesis 3:9–10. When God appeared on the scene, calling for the man, Adam's answer was, *"I heard the sound of you in the garden, and I was afraid, because I was naked, and I hid myself."*

Notice that Adam didn't say, "I did something wrong and didn't want You to find me," but rather, "I'm ashamed because I don't have any fur or feathers to hide behind. I don't want anybody to see me."

Genesis 3:11. *He* [God] *said, "Who told you that you were naked? Have you eaten of the tree of which I commanded you not to eat?"*

That tree held the knowledge of good and evil. Until they ate, they had only known good. Now shame—of the bodies the Lord had given them—became the first evil they met.

Genesis 3:16a. *To the woman he said, "I will surely multiply your pain in childbearing; in pain you shall bring forth children."*

I wonder what would make the act of normal childbirth *more* painful. It would seem that severe pain was one of the side-effects of the fall, but

I wonder if there's more to it than that. If people suddenly needed more space in their brains to judge between evil and good, I can see how that might have resulted in a larger human skull, which in turn would have required more stretching during the birth process.

Genesis 3:16b. "*Your desire shall be _____ your husband,*"

There is disagreement among theologians as to which preposition should fill that blank. Some translations say "*for.*" Several others use "*against.*" Some in each camp have one word in the text and the opposite in a footnote.

H. C. Leupold, an eminent linguist of the twentieth century, renders this phrase "*unto thy husband thou shalt be attracted.*"[1] Beck modernizes this to "*You will long for your husband,*" finishing the passage with "*and he will rule over you.*"

I suspect this desire is why many little girls dream of growing up and getting married, or at least of having children of their own.

Man's rulership, however, does not give him license for abuse. Both men and women need to remember that Eve wasn't created from Adam's foot, so he would walk all over her. She wasn't created from his head, so she could rule over him—though either could have provided sufficient raw material. Instead, God chose to create woman from Adam's rib—a bone specifically designed to protect his heart.

Genesis 3:21. *And the L*ORD *God made for Adam and for his wife garments of skins and clothed them.* God made the first durable clothing at the expense of the lives of two animals—probably pet sheep—from a blood sacrifice to cover their sins. No doubt, they had to watch the killing, knowing that it should have been them.

And God chased them out of the garden.

Genesis 4:1. *Now Adam knew Eve his wife, and she conceived and bore Cain.*

I'm told the original Hebrew spoke rather plainly, as does Beck: *The man had sex relations with his wife Eve, and she conceived and had a child.* Their first child, Cain, killed his next younger sibling. Cain was definitely not the promised Messiah.

LAMECH

Genesis 4:12. Following Abel's murder, Cain became *"a fugitive and a wanderer on the earth."* Adam kept track of the oldest child of the oldest child for several generations, much as parents today will possess many solo pictures of their firstborn but few photos of their other children by themselves.

Genesis 4:19–24. Of Lamech, five generations after Cain, we are told *Lamech took two wives . . . Lamech said to his wives: "Adah and Zillah, hear my voice; you wives of Lamech, listen to what I say: I have killed a man for wounding me, a young man for striking me. If Cain's revenge is sevenfold, then Lamech's is seventy-sevenfold."* Please note in passing that this bully is the first recorded man who had multiple wives. His braggadocios statement that he had *"killed a man for wounding"* him makes me think he was abusive.

NOAH

Genesis 5:1–2. *When God created man, he made him in the likeness of God. Male and female he created them, and he blessed them and named them Man.*

Those words follow what is probably Adam's signature (*toledoth*)[2] to Genesis. I subscribe to the thought that the individual sections of Genesis that are usually translated *"These are the generations of . . ."* actually denote the signatures of separate documents, each authored by the patriarch so credited. Thus, the first *toledoth* ends at Genesis 2:4, marking the prior words as God's statement of creation. Then Genesis 5:1 tells us that the section after 2:4 came from the hand of Adam, who lived through that history. Noah, the author of the next section, recites the lineage of his ancestors all the way back to Adam—information he would have had access to. Moses compiled all those *toledoths* into the book of Genesis, so he was possibly more of an editor than an author, but I'm sure he added comments along the way. Following that, Noah's narrative begins. Notice, again, that humanity was created sexual.

Genesis 6:1–2. *When man began to multiply on the face of the land and daughters were born to them, the sons of God saw that the daughters of man were attractive. And they took as their wives any they chose.*

By this point, men had thousands of choices, but they chose partners on appearance alone.

Genesis 6:4. *The Nephilim were on the earth in those days, and also afterward, when the sons of God came in to the daughters of man and they bore children to them.* Beck calls the Nephilim *tyrants* or *giants*. Apparently, this was one of the signs, or at least results, of the downfall of civilization.

The only cure would be total wipeout by a flood that would cover the entire planet, scrubbing everything clean and totally reorganizing the face of the earth. Only eight people emerged alive—Noah, his wife, his sons Shem, Ham, and Japheth, and their wives. They set foot in a whole new world.

Genesis 9:20–23. Nakedness again. This time Noah, one of the three people God says were His pick of the litter of Old Testament individuals (**Ezekiel 14:14, 20**), got drunk and threw clothes and caution to the winds. His son Ham, possibly accompanied by his grandson Caanan, thought it was funny and tried to make a joke of the situation to Noah's other two sons. They acted to preserve Noah's privacy if not his dignity. Noah, on waking, made it clear that Ham and Caanan's attitudes were wrong, and they ended up receiving a lesser parental blessing.

ABRAM AND SARAI

Jump ahead a few generations to the patriarch Abram, who later became Abraham, and his wife Sarai, whose name would be changed to Sarah, and their extended family:

Genesis 11:30. *Now Sarai was barren; she had no child.*

Sarai, who was not only Abram's wife but also his half-sister, was unable to conceive. The implication is that it wasn't for lack of trying.

Genesis 12:10–13. *Now there was a famine in the land. So Abram went down to Egypt to sojourn there . . . When he was about to enter Egypt, he said to Sarai his wife, "I know that you are a woman beautiful in appearance, and when the Egyptians see you, they will say, 'This is his wife.' Then they will kill me, but they will let you live. Say you are my sister, that it may go well with me because of you, and that my life may be spared for your sake."*

Abram devised a half-truth to save his own skin, apparently not imagining that Sarai might be in any danger.

Genesis 12:14–16. *The Egyptians saw that the woman was very beautiful . . . They praised her to Pharaoh. And the woman was taken into Pharaoh's house. And for her sake he dealt well with Abram; and he had sheep, oxen, male donkeys, male servants, female servants, female donkeys, and camels.*

The Egyptians noticed Sarai's beauty, and suddenly, she was taken into Pharaoh's harem. The ruler even paid Abram lavishly for his "sister."

Genesis 12:17. *But the LORD afflicted Pharaoh and his house with great plagues because of Sarai, Abram's wife.*

Abram definitely had not protected Sarai. So God made intercourse an impossibility with any of the women in the palace. It appears that Pharaoh decided the cause was the new addition to his harem. He questioned Sarai, and she told all.

Genesis 12:18–20. *So Pharaoh called Abram and said, "What is this you have done to me? Why did you not tell me that she was your wife? Why did you say, 'She is my sister,' so that I took her for my wife? Now then, here is your wife; take her, and go." And Pharaoh gave men orders concerning him, and they sent him away with his wife and all that he had.*

Angry, Pharaoh summoned Abram, gave back Sarai, and chased them both out of the country, apparently, letting them keep the "bride price." So although Pharaoh had many wives, he knew it was wrong to take a woman already married to someone else.

ABRAM, SARAI, AND HAGAR

Genesis 16:1–2. *Now Sarai, Abram's wife, had borne him no children. She had a female Egyptian servant whose name was Hagar. And Sarai said to Abram, "Behold now, the LORD has prevented me from bearing children. Go in to my servant; it may be that I shall obtain children by her." And Abram listened to the voice of Sarai.*

Rather than suggesting formal marriage, Sarai was proposing that Hagar become a concubine, not a full-fledged wife.

Abram and Sarai took matters into their own hands rather than trusting God to use the marriage relationship to keep His explicit promise. They started a problem that lingers in the Middle East to this day. It may have been a custom of the time for a barren wife to share her husband, then adopt the child, but it wasn't God's design for family.

Genesis 16:4. *And he went in to Hagar, and she conceived. And when she saw that she had conceived, she looked with contempt on her mistress.*

This proved that it was Sarai, not Abram, who was unable to produce offspring. But sharing a husband started a major feud. Apparently, Sarai was seventy-five when she made the suggestion, which was possibly past her time of menopause.

Genesis 16:5–16. Hagar still belonged to Sarai as her maid, so everybody was miserable at this point. Hagar ran away, God sent her back, then Ishmael was born. Abram was eighty-six.

Genesis 17:10–13. This was the beginning of the practice of circumcision, but it wasn't just a social observance. It was a contract with God. It was to be applied to all males in the community, whether slave or free, starting after they were seven days old. The mark was to be permanent.

Genesis 17:14. *Any uncircumcised male who is not circumcised in the flesh of his foreskin shall be cut off from his people; he has broken my covenant.*

This was serious business.

Genesis 17:15–21. The promise given before was narrowed down to specifics. First, God gave them new names (in Hebrew, names have meanings, so this was really important). The promised child's parents would be Sarah and Abraham, who were ninety and ninety-nine, respectively, at that point. The birth would happen twelve months from the date of this conversation between God (apparently in physical form) and Abraham.

Genesis 17:23–27. Abraham immediately carried out the new directive. He made sure he and Ishmael were circumcised that same day, along with *every male among the men* in his household. We were told in **14:14** that Abraham had 318 male servants born to his household, so Abraham's sphere of influence must have been huge.

Genesis 18:1–10. About three months later, God and two angels appeared visibly to Abraham again. They inquired about Sarah, who was within hearing distance but hidden (from human eyes) inside her tent.

Genesis 18:11–12. *Now Abraham and Sarah were old, advanced in years. The way of women had ceased to be with Sarah. So Sarah laughed to herself, saying, "After I am worn out, and my lord is old, shall I have pleasure?"*

Sarah was definitely past menopause at this point. It sounds like Abraham and Sarah had ceased intercourse, but she had enjoyed that part of their relationship in their earlier days.

Genesis 18:13–15 and **21:1–7.** The promise was repeated. In commemoration of this encounter, the child was named "Laughter."

Genesis 18:16–19. God said not only that He would tell Abraham what was going to happen but that His reason for doing so was so that Abraham *"may command his children and his household after him to keep the way of the LORD by doing righteousness and justice."*

LOT

Genesis 13:13. *Now the men of Sodom were wicked, great sinners against the* LORD.

Jude 1:7 defines the sin of *Sodom and Gomorrah and the surrounding cities,* by saying they *likewise indulged in sexual immorality and pursued unnatural desire.*

This prelude to the story of Lot was given when Abram and Lot separated their households and migrated in different directions. Lot, at first, was living *among the cities of the valley.* Next, he *moved his tent as far as Sodom* in **13:12.** Then, in **14:12,** we discover Lot living in Sodom. In **19:1** he was *sitting in the gate of Sodom,* the meeting place for the leaders of the community.

Genesis 18:20–21. *Then the* LORD *said, "Because the outcry against Sodom and Gomorrah is great and their sin is very grave, I will go down to see whether they have done altogether according to the outcry that has come to me. And if not, I will know."*

Even though God knew what was going on, He still gave the Sodomites their day in court.

Genesis 18:23–32. Abraham bargained with the Lord for Lot's life and well-being. Actually, if Abraham had probably a thousand or more slaves, and the original split between Abraham and Lot had been because they each had more flocks, herds, and servants than available grazing room, in addition to the fact that the two groups of servants didn't get along with each other, then Lot could have had perhaps a hundred servants or more. Thus, to expect that at least ten God-fearing people were in the town— counting Lot, his wife, and their two daughters—should have been a reasonable assumption. Abraham's original request for saving the town if God could find fifty shouldn't have been impossible, for that matter. That the total came down to just four tells us Lot wasn't an influence for good in Sodom. Later, events proved that he had allowed the town to have a very negative impact on his family instead.

Genesis 19:1–3. The angels, posing as men, arrived in Sodom to find Lot sitting in the local equivalent of the town meeting hall/court room. Lot, possibly realizing the danger these "men" would be in, even if he didn't know who they were, invited them to spend the night at his house.

Genesis 19:4–5. *But before they lay down, the men of the city, the men of Sodom, both young and old, all the people to the last man, surrounded the house. And they called to Lot, "Where are the men who came to you tonight? Bring them out to us, that we may know them."*

Again, Beck is more explicit: *"Bring them out to us so we can rape them."*

Note the inclusiveness of their numbers: *all the people to the last man.*

Genesis 19:6–8. *Lot went out to the men at the entrance, shut the door after him, and said, "I beg you, my brothers, do not act so wickedly. Behold, I have two daughters who have not known any man. Let me bring them out to you, and do to them as you please. Only do nothing to these men, for they have come under the shelter of my roof."*

What was Lot thinking? The fact that he didn't stay inside tells us the natives respected him enough that he thought he was safe, at least for the moment. I suspect several of these people were probably his employees.

Lot then identified their proposal as bad behavior, although he didn't use language as strong as God's words. His offer to give them his daughters makes me wonder if he knew there weren't any in that crowd who would be interested in raping women. Yes, the custom of the time said travelers were to be protected and provided for, no matter the inconvenience, but he wasn't doing his daughters any favors.

Genesis 19:9. Sodom's residents replied, *"Stand back . . . This fellow came to sojourn, and he has become the judge! Now we will deal worse with you than with them."* Then they pressed hard against the man Lot, and drew near to break the door down.

The mob turned ugly. It seems they planned to rape Lot—or worse.

Genesis 19:10–11. *But the men* (angels) *reached out their hands and brought Lot into the house with them and shut the door. And they struck with blindness the men who were at the entrance of the house, both small and* *great, so that they wore themselves out groping for the door.*

The angels took over, providing safety for Lot and his family.

Genesis 19:12. *Then the men said to Lot, "Have you anyone else here? Sons-in-law, sons, daughters, or anyone you have in the city, bring them out of the place."*

The angels already knew there weren't ten righteous people. There still should have been two or three who were close friends. Otherwise, we might wonder why Lot even moved into town in the first place.

Genesis 19:13. *"For we are about to destroy this place, because the outcry against its people has become great before the* LORD*, and the* LORD *has sent us to destroy it."*

The coming destruction wasn't because there was a mob that threatened them. It wouldn't be simply as a matter of self-defense. The problem, both in attitudes and actions, had to do with the reason the angels were there in the first place. The angels wouldn't destroy the place via a normal geological event that got somewhat out of hand. Instead, the methodology would be something very rare and unusual.

Genesis 19:14. Lot sneaked out to warn the two men to whom his daughters were engaged. They thought he was *jesting* and ignored the warning.

Genesis 19:15. *As morning dawned, the angels urged Lot, saying, "Up! Take your wife and your two daughters who are here, lest you be swept away in the punishment of the city."*

And still, Lot's family waited, even though their lives were in danger. The angels had arrived the evening before, and Lot's trip out of that safe house to talk to his prospective sons-in-law couldn't have taken long. The logical action would have been to escape under the cover of darkness. I suspect that some serious discussions were needed to even get Lot's own family to be willing to leave the comforts of home.

Genesis 19:16a. *But he lingered.*

Lot had been raised by Abraham, his uncle. He knew better. And still, he was reluctant to leave luxury behind, even knowing that Uncle Abe would probably provide enough for him to start over. He simply didn't believe God would really bring judgment. He may have even reasoned that the "bad" around him in Sodom wasn't really bad after all—strange maybe, but not evil.

Genesis 19:16b. *So the men seized him and his wife and his two daughters by the hand, the Lord being merciful to him, and they brought him out and set him outside the city.*

Genesis 19:17–21. They were cutting it close for time. The angels told Lot to head for the hills, and *"Do not look back or stop anywhere in the valley,"* but Lot didn't even want to go that far. He bargained for them to allow him to take his family into a tiny town—a place perhaps not with the same moral compass as Sodom but still not a community of believers. Even then, he was depending on men, not God, for protection, in spite of what had happened when the mob attacked the previous night.

Genesis 19:23–25. *The sun had risen on the earth when Lot came to Zoar. Then the Lord rained on Sodom and Gomorrah sulfur and fire from the Lord out of heaven. And he overthrew those cities, and all the valley, and all the inhabitants of the cities, and what grew on the ground.*

The opinion of some Bible scholars is that the *sulfur and fire from the Lord* resulted from an eruption of the earth's crust in or near the area now called the Dead Sea.[3] In any case, this natural disaster turned a lush, fertile valley into a barren wasteland. It's obvious that God had been highly incensed with the immorality He found in Sodom and Gomorrah.

Genesis 19:26. *But Lot's wife, behind him, looked back, and she became a pillar of salt.*

I wonder if perhaps she didn't just glance over her shoulder, but rather sat on a rock and watched, mourning over her lost lifestyle. It's possible she preferred death with her new friends to life under God's protection. She died in her rebellion.

Genesis 19:27–29. The thick smoke was visible for miles. God had spared Lot—not because of Lot's actions or because God had a change of heart, but because Lot was important to Abraham. That's grace!

Genesis 19:30. *Now Lot went up out of Zoar and lived in the hills with his two daughters, for he was afraid to live in Zoar. So he lived in a cave with his two daughters.*

This was what the angels had told him to do in the first place. The people of that small town may have blamed Lot for the destruction of their neighbors, or maybe Zoar had the same immoral code as the town he had just left. In any case, Lot became the first cave man mentioned in Scripture.

Genesis 19:31–32. The older daughter suggested to her sister, *"Our father is old, and there is not a man on earth to come in to us after the manner of all the earth. Come, let us make our father drink wine, and we will lie with him, that we may preserve offspring from our father."*

Those young ladies had definitely been affected by the immorality of Sodom.

Genesis 19:33. *So they made their father drink wine that night. And the firstborn went in and lay with her father. He did not know when she lay down or when she arose.*

In a sense, this was date rape in reverse order. In this case, it was also incest.

Genesis 19:34–36. The following day she suggested it was little sister's turn. *So they made their father drink wine that night also. And the younger arose and lay with him, and he did not know when she lay down or when she arose. Thus, both the daughters of Lot became pregnant by their father.*

Same song, second verse. The two resulting sons became the founders of two nations, the Moabites and Ammonites, both of whom were constant enemies of the Israelites for many centuries.

Second Peter 2:6–8 tells us that Lot believed in the God of Abraham. We would have hoped so, as Abraham was Lot's mentor. Therefore, as is true for believers in every time and place, Lot was called upon to be salt and light to the people around him. Instead, he blew it—and lost his whole family in the process.

ABRAHAM AND SARAH

Genesis 20:1–18. The timing here is wild. Sarah would have become pregnant shortly after **18:13–14,** depending on whether or not **21:1–2** is a re-statement of the situation, but in any case, this episode happened quickly. It's understandable that Abraham would want to leave the area of all that destruction. What doesn't make sense is their using the "she's my sister" routine again. Still attractive at ninety, Sarah was taken into the king's harem, where God had to intervene for her protection. Even Abimelech's servants *were very much afraid* when the king told them about his dream. Abraham got a royal chewing out, although Abimelech gave him a substantial gift as a fine for having offended Sarah, Abraham's wife.

Genesis 20:17–18. *Then Abraham prayed to God, and God healed Abimelech, and also healed his wife and female slaves so that they bore children. For the LORD had closed all the wombs of the house of Abimelech because of Sarah, Abraham's wife.*

This might have been a venereal disease. And I can't help but wonder if that's what was visited on the Egyptians when Abraham tried the tactic before.

Genesis 21:1–4. Sarah conceived. Isaac was born. And he was circumcised when he was eight days old (the day after he was a week old), as per the covenant of **17:10–14.**

ISAAC AND REBEKAH

Our focus shifts to the son of Abraham and Sarah, the now-grown-up Isaac.

Genesis 24:2–3. These verses contain a phrase that sounds strange to modern ears: *And Abraham said to his servant . . . who had charge of all that he had, "Put your hand under my thigh, that I may make you swear by* *the LORD, the God of heaven and God of the earth, that you will not take a wife for my son from the daughters of the Canaanites, among whom I dwell."*

As I understand something Dr. Henry M. Morris III stated in *The Book of Beginnings, Volume 3,* I strongly suspect men will form a much more graphic mental picture here than what women would at first envision. The gentlemen are most likely correct in their assumptions. It was a serious oath and needed to be sealed with an action far more intimate than a handshake.[4] **Genesis 24:9** indicates the servant complied with Abraham's request.

The rest of this story contains what we would probably call courting by proxy. Remembering that Isaac and Rebekah were cousins, we note the following passages pertinent to this study:

Genesis 24:16. *The young woman was very attractive in appearance, a maiden whom no man had known.* Beck is more explicit: *She wasn't married—no man had lived with her.*

Genesis 24:58. The arrangements were made almost like a business deal, but Rebekah was given veto power.

Genesis 24:64–65. Recognizing that they were in the right area and about to be officially greeted, Rebekah wanted to make a good first impression. She modestly covered herself with a veil (brides today still follow her lead).

Genesis 24:67. Isaac established her as queen of the household by giving her his mother's tent. Their sharing the tent that night may have been all that was needed to declare them married.

Genesis 25:1–6. It's worthy to note here that Abraham remarried about three years after Sarah's death. Abraham and his new wife, Keturah, had six sons, but she and Hagar were only classified as concubines, not full wives. Thus, Isaac, the son of the true wife, received the bulk of the estate and all the promises from God, especially including the promise of the Messiah.

Genesis 25:21. *And Isaac prayed to the LORD for his wife, because she was barren. And the LORD granted his prayer, and Rebekah his wife conceived.*

Babies do not just happen because a man and a woman have

intercourse. Children are a gift of God. Incidentally, Isaac and Rebekah were married twenty years before their twins were born.

Genesis 26:6–7. *So Isaac settled in Gerar. When the men of the place asked him about his wife, he said, "She is my sister," for he feared to say, "My wife," thinking, "lest the men of the place should kill me because of Rebekah," because she was attractive in appearance.*

Thus, Abraham's subterfuge was tried again for a new generation. In this case, though, it was an outright lie. Rebekah was Isaac's cousin, not his sister.

Genesis 26:8. *When he had been there a long time, Abimelech king of the Philistines looked out of a window and saw Isaac laughing with Rebekah his wife.*

Beck, by contrast, says Abimelech *saw Isaac fondling his wife Rebekah.*

Even after being together for more than twenty years, and with at least one of them now over sixty, Isaac and Rebekah still enjoyed physical intimacy.

Genesis 26:9–11. Abimelech reacted swiftly. *"Behold, she is your wife. How then could you say, 'She is my sister'?" Isaac said to him, "Because I thought, 'Lest I die because of her.'" Abimelech said, "What is this you have done to us? One of the people might easily have lain with your wife, and you would have brought guilt upon us." So Abimelech warned all the people, saying, "Whoever touches this man or his wife shall surely be put to death."*

Often, those who don't worship the God of Abraham know the difference between right and wrong, at least on the broader issues. In any case, unlike Sarah, Rebekah didn't get summoned into the royal harem.

ESAU

Esau, the oldest son of Isaac and Rebekah, doesn't take up much space in Genesis. He didn't seem to really care about things of God—until, that is, twin brother Jacob received not only the spiritual birthright (which Esau had sold to Jacob years earlier) but also the material blessings of wealth and family.

Genesis 26:34–35. *When Esau was forty years old, he took Judith the daughter of Beeri the Hittite to be his wife, and Basemath the daughter of Elon the Hittite, and they made life bitter for Isaac and Rebekah.*

It would seem that, at this point in history, the Hittites were already polytheistic idol worshipers.[5] No wonder those women didn't get along with Isaac and Rebekah.

Genesis 28:6–9. Esau finally got the message that his parents weren't happy with his choices of wives–apparently, he hadn't even noticed the friction before—so he went to Abraham and Hagar's son Ishmael and procured yet a third wife.

JACOB

Even before Esau's third marriage, our focus switches to Jacob and his totally mixed up family.

Genesis 28:1–3. Isaac sent Jacob to Paddan-aram, to Rebekah's father, to find a wife among the daughters of his Uncle Laban. Jacob was dispatched with this benediction: *"God Almighty bless you and make you fruitful and multiply you, that you may become a company of peoples."*

It wouldn't be an arranged marriage, as Isaac and Rebekah's had been, but would be one with someone who, the parents hoped, was still a believer.

Genesis 29:16–18. Laban had two daughters. *Leah's eyes were weak, but Rachel was beautiful in form and appearance. Jacob loved Rachel. And he said, "I will serve you seven years for your younger daughter Rachel."*

Jacob had been sent there specifically to find a bride among Laban's daughters. He made his choice by the end of the first month.

Genesis 29:20. *So Jacob served seven years for Rachel, and they seemed to him but a few days because of the love he had for her.*

No matter how much actual courtship occurred, Jacob was excitedly enjoying the anticipation.

Genesis 29:21–23. *Then Jacob said to Laban, "Give me my wife that I may go in to her, for my time is completed." So Laban gathered together all the people of the place and made a feast. But in the evening he took his daughter Leah and brought her to Jacob, and he went in to her.*

The reception was apparently held before the ceremony—or perhaps there wasn't a ceremony in those days; maybe they just went into the tent together and had intercourse. I wonder if this incident is why, in present-day marriage vows, the bride and groom always state their names.

Genesis 29:25. *And in the morning, behold, it was Leah! And Jacob said to Laban, "What is this you have done to me? Did I not serve with you for Rachel? Why then have you deceived me?"*

The one I feel sorry for is Leah. She had to do a credible job of pretending to be her sister—all night—and still might have wondered if she would be thrown out—or worse—in the morning. I get the feeling that she may have liked Jacob, but she'd probably always been living in the shadow of her vivacious sister. I also suspect that Leah knew the promises from God that went with being Jacob's wife, and she wanted that legacy—enough to go along with the pretense. In the final analysis, the choice wasn't only Laban's, it was God's.

Genesis 29:26–27. *Laban said, "It is not so done in our country, to give the younger before the firstborn. Complete the week of this one, and we will give you the other also in return for serving me another seven years."*

"Complete the week" probably meant the newlyweds had the entire week of vacation and were expected to spend their time in the bedroom/tent. In any case, the implication is that Jacob and Leah had indeed had intercourse, therefore, they were married, even if she wasn't who he thought she was.

Genesis 29:28. *Jacob did so, and completed her week. Then Laban gave him his daughter Rachel to be his wife.*

At this point, Jacob had two wives and a labor contract he couldn't get out of for seven more years.

Genesis 29:30. *So Jacob went in to Rachel also, and he loved Rachel more than Leah, and served Laban for another seven years.*

We can imagine the friction. Not only are there two wives, regarded very unequally, they're sisters. The conflict of their two temperaments just continued on to a new level.

Genesis 29:31. *When the LORD saw that Leah was hated, he opened her womb, but Rachel was barren.*

It appears that Jacob continued marital relations with both wives, but Rachel got the lion's share of his time and attention. Rachel became more jealous with each new pregnancy. No matter the human actions, God was still in control.

Genesis 29:32–35. Leah and Jacob had four sons in possibly eight years. *Then she* [Leah] *ceased bearing.* Actually, Leah only stopped bearing for a while. She later had two more sons and a daughter. Rachel still hadn't become pregnant.

Genesis 30:1. *When Rachel saw that she bore Jacob no children, she envied her sister. She said to Jacob, "Give me children, or I shall die!"*

That sounds a bit melodramatic. She'd had Jacob in her tent probably the majority of the time, yet she blamed him for not visiting often enough.

Genesis 30:2. *Jacob's anger was kindled against Rachel, and he said, "Am I in the place of God, who has withheld from you the fruit of the womb?"*

Jacob, at least, knew that children are a gift from God. After all, he and Esau weren't born until after their parents had been married twenty years.

Genesis 30:3–4. *Then she said, "Here is my servant Bilhah; go in to her, so that she may give birth on my behalf, that even I may have children through her." So she gave him her servant Bilhah as a wife, and Jacob went in to her.*

This sounds like Sarah and Hagar, revisited. Jacob now had a harem, almost.

Genesis 30:5–8. Their co-habiting wasn't just a one-time thing. Jacob and Bilhah had two sons.

Genesis 30:9–13. Then Leah copied her sister and offered her maid Zilpah as a concubine. Jacob and Zilpah had two sons.

Genesis 30:14–15. One summer, *Reuben went and found mandrakes in the field and brought them to his mother Leah. Then Rachel said to Leah, "Please give me some of your son's mandrakes." But she said to her, "Is it a small matter that you have taken away my husband? Would you take away my son's mandrakes also?" Rachel said, "Then he may lie with you tonight in exchange for your son's mandrakes."*

Reuben was the oldest son. According to *Easton's Bible Dictionary*, mandrakes are classified as nightshades, which are in the same category as potatoes and tomatoes. They also state, "It possesses stimulating and narcotic properties."[6]

Genesis 30:16. *When Jacob came from the field in the evening, Leah went out to meet him and said, "You must come in to me, for I have hired you with my son's mandrakes." So he lay with her that night.*

And the act that was designed by God as an expression of love became merely a commercial transaction. Among God-fearing people, no less.

Genesis 30:17–18. *And God listened to Leah, and she conceived and bore Jacob a fifth son. Leah said, "God has given me my wages because I gave my servant to my husband." So she called his name Issachar.*

Leah rightly understood God's hand in procreation, she just cited the wrong reason. Some Bible translations offer the meaning of the child's name as "Reward," others as "There Is Hire." Imagine a child growing up with the knowledge that his mother had to pay to get her husband to sleep with her!

Think about what must have been going through Reuben's mind. The boy was probably a teenager when he brought his mother that gift, feeling sorry for her since she apparently received little positive attention in Jacob's household. Mom gave his gift to Aunt Rachel, who had been getting all the good stuff in the first place. His reward, nine months later, was another little brother. Some days, life just doesn't seem fair.

Genesis 30:19–21. *And Leah conceived again, and she bore Jacob a sixth son. Then Leah said, ". . . now my husband will honor me, because I have borne him six sons." So she called his name Zebulun. Afterward she bore a daughter and called her name Dinah.*

Jacob must not have totally neglected Leah, but she wasn't his top pick for any evening.

Genesis 30:22–24. *Then God remembered Rachel, and God listened to her and opened her womb. She conceived and bore a son and said, "God has taken away my reproach." And she called his name Joseph, saying, "May the LORD add to me another son!"*

Thus, Joseph was possibly twenty years younger than Reuben.

The remainder of **Genesis 30** contains a lesson in animal husbandry. Basically, it reminds us that God is the one in charge of DNA distribution, in animals as well as in humans. The net result of this chapter is that Jacob obtained as his wages the more valuable sheep and goats while Laban, who thought he was once again cheating his son-in-law, ended up with the weaker animals.

Jacob decided his years of servitude to Laban had been fulfilled. He, therefore, took his complicated family (including eleven sons and one daughter), his flocks, herds, and servants and headed back toward what is now the country of Israel. He did so rather quickly and without warning to Laban or Laban's sons, who had moved their camp north a three-day march so Jacob couldn't steal any of their animals.

Genesis 31:19. *Laban had gone to shear his sheep, and Rachel stole her father's household gods.* This has nothing, directly, to do with sex. It has everything to do with attitudes. Rachel was willing to go with Jacob back to his far-away home, where Aunt Rebekah had lived, but she wasn't willing to part with the idols her parents had worshiped. And *that* was why God chose

Leah, rather than Rachel, to be Jacob's first wife—the one to bear the children whose offspring would lead the spiritual life of the nation (Levi and Judah), and many generations later, to be an ancestress of the Messiah, Jesus.

Genesis 31:20–33. Laban heard about it three days later (after all, he was the one who had moved what he thought was the good flock that far away, out of Jacob's reach). He rounded up the rest of the clan and went in hot pursuit. Laban had also discovered that those family idols were missing. Apparently, they were as important to him as daughters and grandchildren. Jacob, not knowing about Rachel's actions, offered to execute anybody who had stolen *anything* that belonged to Laban. So Laban searched Jacob's tent, Leah's, Bilhah's, Zilpah's, and then entered Rachel's.

Genesis 31:34–35. Rachel hid those stolen idols in her camel's saddle and sat on them. Then, while Laban searched her tent, she told him, *"Let not my lord be angry that I cannot arise before you, for the way of women is upon me."* So he searched but did not find the household gods.

Again, Beck is a whole lot plainer: *"I can't get up in front of you. I'm having my period."*

I wonder if she was always a spoiled brat? In any case, her trick worked. Laban gave up the search and went back home.

DINAH

Jacob and his entourage arrived in the land God had promised to Abraham. They settled for a few years in Succoth.

Genesis 34:1–2. Dinah, the youngest child of Leah and Jacob, *went out to see the women of the land. And when Shechem the son of Hamor the Hivite, the prince of the land, saw her, he seized her and lay with her and humiliated her.*

Beck says he raped her. Dinah and Joseph may have been about the same age, as both were born shortly before they escaped from Laban. In any case, she wasn't very old, perhaps barely a teenager at this time. The perpetrator was the son of the village chief.

Genesis 34:3–4. *And his soul was drawn to Dinah the daughter of Jacob. He loved the young woman and spoke tenderly to her. So Shechem spoke to his father Hamor, saying, "Get me this girl for my wife."*

Shechem raped Dinah, apparently not bothering to woo her first. His attitude was all about his wants. I sense all sorts of bad things going on here.

Genesis 34:5. *Now Jacob heard that he had defiled his daughter Dinah. But his sons were with his livestock in the field, so Jacob held his peace until they came.*

Apparently, all this time, Dinah was in Shechem's home, whether by force or consent.

Genesis 34:6–7. Hamor, Shechem's father, came to bargain with Jacob. All Dinah's brothers arrived *as soon as they heard of it, and the men were indignant and very angry, because he had done an outrageous thing in Israel by lying with Jacob's daughter, for such a thing must not be done.*

The older boys were probably in their twenties or even thirties. Their little sister had been violated, and they were furious.

Genesis 34:8–10. So Hamor proposed a treaty: *"The soul of my son Shechem longs for your daughter. Please give her to him to be his wife. Make marriages with us. Give your daughters to us, and take our daughters for yourselves. You shall dwell with us, and the land shall be open to you. Dwell and trade in it, and get property in it."*

Hamor must have been a politician. His proposal sounded more like a business deal—the first of many.

Genesis 34:11–12. *Shechem also said to her father and to her brothers, "Let me find favor in your eyes, and whatever you say to me I will give. Ask me for as great a bride-price and gift as you will, and I will give whatever you say to me. Only give me the young woman to be my wife."*

It seems that Shechem hadn't learned to control his raging teenage hormones and was used to getting whatever he wanted.

Genesis 34:13. *The sons of Jacob answered Shechem and his father Hamor deceitfully, because he had defiled their sister Dinah.*

What they meant was, "You raped; we kill." Notice that it was Dinah's brothers, not her father, who set the conditions.

Genesis 34:14–17. The brothers answered, *"We cannot do this thing, to give our sister to one who is uncircumcised, for that would be a disgrace to us. Only on this condition will we agree with you—that you will become as we are by every male among you being circumcised. Then we will give our daughters to you, and we will take your daughters to ourselves, and we will dwell with you and become one people. But if you will not listen to us and be circumcised, then we will take our daughter, and we will be gone."*

The bottom line is, if all the males weren't circumcised, they would be considered unclean and thus not eligible suitors. They got that part right. The greater problem was that these people belonged to the same tribe as Esau's first two wives. Thus, they were idol worshipers whose influences were supposed to be avoided.

Genesis 34:18–19. *Their words pleased Hamor and Hamor's son Shechem. And the young man did not delay to do the thing, because he delighted in Jacob's daughter. Now he was the most honored of all his father's house.*

In other words, Shechem was still infatuated with Dinah. He was positive he was a great catch—a combination of Prince Charming and heir apparent. In reality, he was a spoiled rich kid.

Genesis 34:20–24. Hamor and Shechem sold the idea to the rest of their town, presenting it as a business opportunity. They convinced them, for every man and boy, *all who went out of the gate of his city,* was circumcised.

Genesis 34:25. *On the third day, when they were sore, two of the sons of Jacob, Simeon and Levi, Dinah's brothers, took their swords and came against the city while it felt secure and killed all the males.*

Thus, not Reuben, the oldest son of Jacob and Leah, but the two next younger brothers carried out their revenge, not just on Shechem and his family, but on the entire village.

Genesis 34:26. *They killed Hamor and his son Shechem with the sword and took Dinah out of Shechem's house and went away.*

And they made sure their sister arrived safely back home.

Genesis 34:27. *The sons of Jacob came upon the slain and plundered the city, because they had defiled their sister.*

This part of the retaliation may have included Reuben, Judah, and perhaps even some of the younger brothers. They might have heard that some of the other boys of the neighborhood were making improper advances toward their sister Dinah, since the entire town received the punishment. To say her brothers were incensed would be an understatement.

Genesis 34:28–30. Having killed all the men and boys, the brothers now took not just animals and wealth, but women and children as well. Jacob realized this was overkill and worried that other Hittites might call for revenge. The brothers had other concerns:

Genesis 34:31. *But they said, "Should he treat our sister like a prostitute?"*

It was time to move on.

Genesis 35:2–3. Jacob told his family and servants, *"Put away the foreign gods that are among you and purify yourselves and change your garments. Then let us arise and go up to Bethel, so that I may make there an altar to the God who answers me in the day of my distress and has been with me wherever I have gone."*

Again, this is not a sexual statement but one of attitude: clean out all the dirt and prepare to worship God. Even their earrings were discarded, along with the idols Rachel had stolen.

Genesis 35:16–20. Rachel apparently had become pregnant again, finally, while they were living in Succoth. As they moved their camp south, she went into difficult labor and died giving birth to Benjamin. It's highly possible that Leah became responsible for raising both Benjamin and his full brother, Joseph—both of whom were the sons of her rival for Jacob's attention.

Our focus widens to include highlights (in this case, more properly low-lights) from the grown-up lives of Jacob's sons.

Genesis 35:22. *While Israel lived in that land, Reuben went and lay with Bilhah his father's concubine. And Israel heard of it.*

The family settled in the area which is now Bethlehem. Reuben, the oldest son of Jacob and Leah, probably by now in his late twenties, either raped or seduced (or was seduced by) Bilhah, his Aunt Rachel's maid. Leah, Rachel, and Bilhah were all also wives of his father, Jacob. Talk about a dysfunctional family.

JOSEPH

Genesis 37:3–4. *Now Israel loved Joseph more than any other of his sons, because he was the son of his old age. And he made him a robe of many colors. But when his brothers saw that their father loved him more than all his brothers, they hated him and could not speak peacefully to him.*

Family relationships still had major problems, even though sex was no longer the main issue. I strongly suspect Joseph reminded Jacob of Rachel—the wife he had loved the most. In any case, the dysfunction continued.

The older brothers captured Joseph (Rachel's oldest son) and sold him to the next trading caravan that showed up, who then re-sold him to a high official in Egypt. Most of the remainder of Genesis deals with the life of Joseph, except for the rather complicated saga of Judah (the fourth son of Leah and an ancestor of Jesus).

JUDAH AND TAMAR

Genesis 38:1–6. Judah seems to have been fed up with all the family problems. He struck off on his own, marrying a Canaanite woman with whom he had three sons. Following the practice of arranged marriages, Judah picked Tamar to marry his oldest son.

Genesis 38:7. *But Er, Judah's firstborn, was wicked in the sight of the* LORD, *and the* LORD *put him to death.*

We aren't told what Er did that was so bad, just that he died without offspring.

Genesis 38:8. *Then Judah said to Onan, "Go in to your brother's wife and perform the duty of a brother-in-law to her, and raise up offspring for your brother."*

Centuries later, this standing custom was actually written into Mosaic Law in **Deuteronomy 25:5–6.**

Genesis 38:9–10. *But Onan knew that the offspring would not be his. So whenever he went in to his brother's wife he would waste the semen on the ground, so as not to give offspring to his brother. And what he did was wicked in the sight of the* LORD, *and he put him to death also.*

Never let it be said that the Bible isn't plain spoken. Onan didn't mind having sex with Tamar, as long as it was on his terms.

Genesis 38:11. *Then Judah said to Tamar his daughter-in-law, "Remain a widow in your father's house, till Shelah my son grows up"—for he feared that he would die, like his brothers. So Tamar went and remained in her father's house.*

I can almost hear the thoughts churning through Judah's mind, "There has to be something wrong with this girl. It's not possible that both of my grown-up sons would have had problems. I'll send her back home, hoping she gets tired of waiting and marries somebody else." To Tamar, he said, effectively, "We'll call you when we need you."

Genesis 38:12. After a while Judah's wife died. Once the mourning period was over, Judah went back to business as usual—shearing the sheep and throwing a party.

Genesis 38:13–14. *And when Tamar was told, "Your father-in-law is going up to Timnah to shear his sheep," she took off her widow's garments and covered herself with a veil, wrapping herself up, and sat . . . on the road to Timnah. For she* *saw that Shelah was grown up, and she had not been given to him in marriage.*

Like Leah before her, Tamar had apparently absorbed enough information about the unique blessing being passed from generation to generation in Judah's family to know that she wanted to be part of that picture. She had determined that she would do almost anything to stay included. Thus, when her sources reported that Judah was ignoring her, she kept track of his movements and devised a scheme to get his attention.

Whether mourning clothes were black in that day, or otherwise distinctive, they were far different from the outfit of a cult prostitute she ended up donning, which perhaps consisted of little more than a long veil of some flimsy, opaque fabric she could wrap herself in from head to toe.

Genesis 38:15. *When Judah saw her, he thought she was a prostitute, for she had covered her face.*

Judah had apparently decided that however short the time since his wife had died, he was ready for some sex. And there, beside the road, sat a shapely woman whom Judah assumed was one of the prostitutes who were a standard part of idol worship in many of the religions of that era. Thus, knowing that dealing with a prostitute was wrong, Judah decided he had found just what he needed to put him in a party mood. He, no doubt, reasoned that one quick fling couldn't hurt anything.

Genesis 38:16. *He turned to her at the roadside and said, "Come, let me come in to you," for he did not know that she was his daughter-in-law. She said, "What will you give me, that you may come in to me?"*

Tamar's disguise had worked. Judah requested to rent her body for a short time.

Genesis 38:17. *He answered, "I will send you a young goat from the flock." And she said, "If you give me a pledge, until you send it—"*

Tamar knew she would need something for evidence. Obviously, DNA testing didn't exist yet. Judah offered a goat, which would be delivered the next day. The problem was, he could have conveniently forgotten to follow through. She needed something much more distinctive than an animal anyway.

Genesis 38:18. *He said, "What pledge shall I give you?" She replied, "Your signet and your cord and your staff that is in your hand." So he gave them to her and went in to her, and she conceived by him.*

This was a rather bold request. The staff was used in sorting sheep, so he probably wouldn't need that at the party. His seal, however, was his distinctive imprinter for business deals—almost the equivalent of handing her his debit card. Judah certainly wasn't thinking clearly, which is exactly what Tamar had hoped. It was dark in the tent, so he didn't discover her identity.

Genesis 38:19. Probably the minute Judah left, Tamar slipped into her widow's weeds again and made a fast exit in the other direction.

Genesis 38:20. *When Judah sent the young goat by his friend the Adullamite to take back the pledge from the woman's hand, he did not find her.*

Judah had never intended to see the woman again when he hired her services. By the time Hiram arrived with a goat to make the payoff, Tamar was long gone.

Genesis 38:21–23. Hiram asked around a bit, specifically for the sacred prostitute, and was told there had never been such a person at that location. Judah, perhaps realizing the trouble he would be in with father Jacob if the story got out that he had been intimate with a woman whose sexual exploits were part of a pagan worship ritual, told Hiram that it wasn't worth further inquiry.

Genesis 38:24. *About three months later Judah was told, "Tamar your daughter-in-law has been immoral. Moreover, she is pregnant by immorality." And Judah said, "Bring her out, and let her be burned."*

More than likely, the village gossips told Judah that Tamar had been a prostitute and now she was with child. I can easily imagine that Judah thought, "I was hoping this would happen. Now we can legally get rid of this hooker before she contaminates my son Shelah, and then we can proceed to find him a decent wife. I knew there was something wrong with that woman, right from the start."

Genesis 38:25. *As she was being brought out, she sent word to her father-in-law, "By the man to whom these belong, I am pregnant." And she said, "Please identify whose these are, the signet and the cord and the staff."*

She had him—publicly. There was no way he could deny what he had done.

Genesis 38:26. *Then Judah identified them and said, "She is more righteous than I, since I did not give her to my son Shelah." And he did not know her again.*

Lest there be any doubt as to the relationship, let's augment the euphemism so often employed in English Bibles. The ESV translation may be word-for-word perfect, but Beck leaves no doubt as to the meaning: *He didn't have intercourse with her again.* Judah had to accept her as part of his household, although not as a wife. But while Judah pushed her off to a corner and probably tried to totally ignore her, God had heard Tamar's desire to be part of the family of the special promise. She is the first of only four women mentioned by Matthew as ancestresses of Jesus.

Genesis 38:27–30. Tamar gave birth to twins, so Judah still had three sons to pass on his legacy. A brief recap also appears in **1 Chronicles 2:3–4.**

JOSEPH

And now back to Joseph, who was doing well in his new environment:

Genesis 39:6–7. *Now Joseph was handsome in form and appearance. And after a time his master's wife cast her eyes on Joseph and said, "Lie with me."*

Joseph was successfully functioning as chief executive officer of Potiphar's household when Potiphar's wife attempted to seduce him.

Genesis 39:8–9. Joseph refused her advances, telling her, *"Behold, because of me my master has no concern about anything in the house, and he has put everything that he has in my charge. He is not greater in this house than I am, nor has he kept back anything from me except you, because you* *are his wife. How then can I do this great wickedness and sin against God?"*

Potiphar and Joseph had probably never even discussed the potential of sexual relations between servant and wife. Both rightly assumed it was a given that she was off-limits. For Joseph, the reason to refuse her advances had a more important aspect—the line that God had drawn Himself: *Thou shalt not* (KJV).

Genesis 39:10. *And as she spoke to Joseph day after day, he would not listen to her, to lie beside her or to be with her.*

Joseph became cautious in his activities. He probably made sure another servant was with him at all times whenever he was called into rooms where she might be.

Genesis 39:11. *But one day, when he went into the house to do his work and none of the men of the house was there in the house . . .*

Just once, Joseph let down his guard. It's highly possible that Potiphar's wife had sent her personal servants on errands to the far corners of the estate. In any case, her trap was set.

Genesis 39:12. *She caught him by his garment, saying, "Lie with me." But he left his garment in her hand and fled and got out of the house.*

Her ambush was arranged. She probably suddenly popped out of hiding, perhaps coming up behind him. She thought she had him. Joseph, realizing that evasive action wouldn't work, abandoned his garment (whether uniform jacket or everything he had on) and ran back outside.

Genesis 39:13–15. When Potiphar's wife realized she clutched an empty garment, for Joseph had successfully evaded her and escaped outdoors, *she called to the men of her household and said to them, "See, he has brought among us a Hebrew to laugh at us. He came in to me to lie with me, and I cried out with a loud voice. And as soon as he heard that I lifted up my voice and cried out, he left his garment beside me and fled and got out of the house."*

There is an expression, "Hell hath no fury like a woman scorned." If this woman couldn't get what she wanted, then she would certainly do all in her power to punish Joseph. She probably *had* started screaming the moment she realized she was left with an empty coat. But her screams were screams of rage, not pleas for help. Notice the hint she planned to drop, that it was really Potiphar's fault. After all, "*He . . . brought . . . the Hebrew.*"

Genesis 39:16–18. Holding onto her evidence until Potiphar returned home, *she told him the same story, saying, "The Hebrew servant, whom you have brought among us, came in to me to laugh at me. But as soon as I lifted up my voice and cried, he left his garment beside me and fled out of the house."*

Beck has her saying Joseph came to her "*to make love to*" her. No doubt, she made sure the servants would see to it that Potiphar talked to her before Joseph had a chance to present his side of the story. She had plenty of time to practice the lie, complete with the expected emotions.

Genesis 39:19–20. When Potiphar heard her accusation, "*This is the way your servant treated me," his anger was kindled. And Joseph's master took him and put him into the prison, the place where the king's prisoners were confined, and he was there in prison.*

Potiphar had to do something. It's highly possible he was more angry at his wife and at the necessity of losing his most gifted chief executive officer, than he ever was at Joseph. Although he may have observed some of his wife's advances (and Joseph's reactions) before that fateful day, it was still the word of a woman with significant social standing against the word of a foreign slave. H. C. Leupold said that if Potiphar had really believed her story, he would have had Joseph executed immediately.[7] Instead, he saw to it that this trusted servant was housed in the cushiest prison in the land.

It may have seemed that everything was going wrong in Joseph's life, but God needed to move him to that prison in order to pave his way to the court of Pharaoh, where Joseph so amazed them with his God-given wisdom that he was appointed chief executive officer of the entire land of Egypt.

Genesis 41:45. *And Pharaoh called Joseph's name Zaphenath-paneah. And he gave him in marriage Asenath, the daughter of Potiphera priest of On.*

And so we see another arranged marriage. Unfortunately, this daughter of a pagan priest seems to have had a negative influence on their descendants, even though the Lord blessed those tribes because of the faithfulness of their ancestor Joseph.

The drought Joseph had predicted for Egypt was causing great problems in Canaan as well. Jacob sent ten of his sons to Egypt to buy grain. The men didn't realize they were dealing with their own brother, for he looked like an Egyptian and spoke to them through an interpreter. Joseph demanded that they bring their youngest brother (his full brother Benjamin) back with them the next time they came looking for grain.

Genesis 42:38. *But he* [Jacob] *said, "My son shall not go down with you, for his brother is dead, and he is the only one left. If harm should happen to him on the journey that you are to make, you would bring down my gray hairs with sorrow to Sheol."*[8]

Jacob still thought of Rachel as his only real wife.

Joseph revealed himself to his brothers, forgave them for what they had done to him, and insisted that the entire family pull up roots and re-settle in Egypt to ride out the famine.

JACOB IN EGYPT

Only a few remaining excerpts are pertinent to our subject:

Genesis 46:10. Simeon had six sons. We are told that the youngest was *the son of a Canaanite woman.* That would have to mean that Simeon's other wife was not a local native. I wonder if that might indicate that Simeon married his sister, Dinah. She is listed in **46:15** as one of Jacob's descendants who traveled with them to Egypt.

Genesis 46:17. The only two female descendants of Jacob listed among those immigrants were Dinah (daughter of Jacob and Leah) and Serah (daughter of Asher, thus granddaughter of Jacob and Zilpah). I wonder if Serah perhaps married a cousin? Of seventy-one named children and grandchildren, all but two were male. Remember that thought when you discover the size of the community of the Exodus.

Genesis 49:3–4. "*Reuben, you are my firstborn, my might, and the first-fruits of my strength . . . Unstable as water, you shall not have preeminence, because you went up to your father's bed; then you defiled it—he went up to my couch!*"

Reuben, the oldest son of Leah and Jacob, was possibly in his early thirties when the incident with Bilhah occurred—old enough that his father decided it wouldn't do any good at that time to try to correct him. At this point, Jacob was on his deathbed, giving his patriarchal blessing to each of his sons, and he hadn't forgotten.

Genesis 49:25–26. "*By the God of your father who will help you, by the Almighty, who will bless you with blessings of heaven above, blessings of the deep that crouches beneath, blessings of the breasts and of the womb. The blessings of your father are mighty beyond the blessings of my parents, up to the bounties of the everlasting hills. May they be on the head of Joseph, and on the brow of him who was set apart from his brothers.*"

Jacob gave Joseph the most generous blessings, which included not only natural resources but also large families. Indeed, the tribes of Ephraim and Manasseh were leaders of what became the Northern Kingdom of Israel.

From the creation of Adam and Eve to the death of the patriarch Jacob, God's Word in Genesis reveals to us a glimpse of what God intended sex to be, but we've also seen some of the severe problems that occur when people try their own variations.

And we've only just begun.

2

THE BASIC RULES
AND REGS

EXODUS 1:8–12. IN THE roughly 400 years between Genesis and the exodus from Egypt, the group that started with twelve sons of Jacob would number 600,000 men, plus women and children. Called "Hebrews" now, they were still in Egypt, trapped there as slaves. The country was ruled by a pharaoh who didn't care what position some character named Joseph had held under prior administrations. He needed slaves to build his pyramid, monuments, and cities, so in order to keep them always in subjection, he set taskmasters over them to make their work even harder. But that didn't solve his problem. They just kept multiplying.

Exodus 1:15–16 (Beck). *Then the king of Egypt talked to the Hebrew midwives . . . "When you help the Hebrew women give birth to a child, examine the child . . . If it is a boy, kill him; if it is a girl, let her live."*

Pharaoh decided the easiest way to keep his workers, but stop their tribe from increasing, would be to simply kill their infant sons. It would be as though a ruler, in our time, ordered DNA testing during pregnancy. If the tests discovered a Y chromosome, the baby would be aborted.

Exodus 1:17 (Beck). *But the midwives feared God and didn't do what the king of Egypt told them; they let the boys live.*

The midwives (nurses specially trained to deliver babies) decided the law was immoral, so they refused to kill the baby boys. They lied to Pharaoh, telling him the infants were already born by the time they were called in. Because the midwives chose to obey God rather than Pharaoh, God blessed them with large families.

Exodus 1:22 (Beck). So Pharaoh ordered, *"Throw every Hebrew boy that is born into the river . . . but let every girl live."*

Foiled in his original plan, the ruler, just like King Herod, ordered infanticide for all boy babies, and anyone could kill them.

MOSES

Exodus 2:1–6. During the time of the edict to drown the boy babies, Moses was born into a family of Levi's descendants. His mother hid him for three months, then placed him in a waterproof basket and secreted it in the weeds close to the bank of the Nile. His sister hid nearby so she could keep track of what happened to her little brother. Pharaoh's daughter discovered the basket and thus the child, but instead of killing this little Hebrew boy, she decided she wanted to keep him as her own.

Exodus 2:7 (Beck). At that, Miriam came out of hiding. *"Should I go and call a nursing woman of the Hebrews to nurse the baby for you?"*

There was just one problem: a human mother only produces milk after her baby is born. Once that child stops nursing, the flow soon stops. And baby bottles hadn't been invented yet. Thus, the royal princess and her attendants had no way to feed this baby. But big sister came to the rescue!

Exodus 2:8–10 (Beck). Pharaoh's daughter may have guessed who Miriam had in mind, but the idea had merit. The nurse Miriam brought was, of course, Moses' mother. Pharaoh's daughter instructed her, *"Take this child . . . nurse him for me, and I will pay you."*

The woman took the child and nursed him. When the child had grown, she brought him to Pharaoh's daughter, and he became her son. She called him Moses, saying, "It is because I took him out of the water."

Thus, for his first few years, Moses was actually raised by his own parents, in his own family. Then he was formally adopted by Pharaoh's daughter.

Exodus 2:11–22. Moses grew up as a junior member of Pharaoh's court but got in trouble for killing an Egyptian guard who was beating a Hebrew man. Moses escaped to the land of Midian, where, much like Jacob, he took a job as a shepherd and married the owner's daughter.

Moses and his wife, Zipporah, had a son while in Midian.

Exodus 3:1—4:17. Then one day God spoke to Moses from Mount Sinai out of a bush that flamed but didn't burn up. God gave Moses a mission: return to Egypt, free the Hebrews from Egyptian rule, and bring God's people back to that mountain so they could worship Him there.

Exodus 4:18–23. Moses and his little family headed for Egypt. There was, however, one detail that had to be taken care of first:

Exodus 4:24–26 (Beck). *While they were at a lodging place on the way, the LORD met him and tried to kill him. Then Zipporah took a flint-stone knife, cut off her son's foreskin, and laid it at his feet. "You are a bride-groom by blood to me!" she said. So God let him alone.*

Moses had neglected to perform the rite of circumcision for one of his two sons when they were infants, so he wasn't allowed to proceed any further until that was taken care of. His wife Zipporah actually did the surgery, using a stone knife.

Exodus 4:27—11:3. Moses' older brother Aaron met him en route, and together they returned to Egypt. God orchestrated a series of major disasters, affecting not only the Egyptians' crops but also their animals and their own physical health. Pharaoh, however, refused to let the Hebrews even have a week's vacation, let alone leave the country. It was time for one final plague:

Exodus 11:4–5 (Beck). *Moses said, "The LORD says: 'At midnight I will go out among the Egyptians, and every firstborn in Egypt will die, from the firstborn of Pharaoh sitting on his throne to the firstborn of the slave girl behind the handmill, and also every firstborn among the cattle.'"*

Pharaoh had attempted to kill the leadership of a generation of Hebrews by murdering all the male babies. God cut off the leadership of

Egypt for several generations by killing all their firstborn, both infants and aged, extending even to their cattle, thus destroying any remaining wealth of Egypt. Pharaoh would be left with greatly reduced resources, making it difficult for him to re-enslave the escaping Hebrews.

Exodus 14. Of course, the armies of Pharaoh did try to overtake and punish their former slaves, so God opened a pathway for exodus of His people right through the middle of the Red Sea. Then God drowned soldiers, chariots, and horses when He closed the waters back over the Egyptians. In commemoration of that event, a special ceremony was initiated that is still practiced by Jews today. Called Passover, it has some distinct rules that relate to our subject matter.

Exodus 12:43–49 (Beck). "*No foreigner should eat of it. Any slave, bought for money, may eat of it after you have circumcised him . . . If a stranger is staying with you and wants to celebrate the Passover for the LORD, all his males should be circumcised . . .*" making him like a native-born citizen. "*But no uncircumcised person should eat of it. A stranger who lives among you is bound by the same law as anyone born in Israel.*"

It would seem that God took circumcision very seriously.

THE COMMANDMENTS

Forty years passed from the time they left Egypt to Moses' death at the end of Deuteronomy. In that interval, of those who were twenty or older when they crossed the Red Sea, all but three died in the wilderness. They were replaced by probably two generations of their descendants. Thus, the rules and regulations God gave the people at Mount Sinai needed to be repeated for those new generations.

Before we delve further into those statutes, a few unfamiliar phrases and expressions applicable to our topic, could use some clarification. Many other Bible translations avoid using some words, instead falling back on King

James English so as not to offend anyone. If you are verifying this book's quotations with another Scripture translation, you will often find there the phrases "*to lie with*" or "*to uncover the nakedness of,*" both of which denote sexual intercourse. Another archaic phrase you might encounter there is "*to whore after,*" which means to act like a prostitute. The quotations in this chapter come from *An American Translation* (otherwise known as simply "Beck"),[9] which is, like the original Hebrew, much more plain-spoken than most other versions. Thus, there will be no question here as to those meanings.

There are several regulations for occasions after which the following expression appears: "*and be unclean till evening*" (Beck). This meant that, for that time frame, the person so affected could not enter the tabernacle (and later the temple or a synagogue), nor were they allowed to touch sacred items. They would also have been barred from celebrations such as Passover and family Sabbath observances—quarantined even within their own household.

I have combined and condensed the laws that deal with sex and related issues in the books of **Exodus**, **Leviticus**, **Numbers**, and **Deuteronomy**. For the most part, I have used Moses' organization, listing different items in the order they are first mentioned. But before we get into the details, let's start with the pertinent commandments.

Exodus 20:14 and **Deuteronomy 5:18** (Beck). "*Do not commit adultery.*"

Most of the other commandments are easy to understand. If someone is lying dead in the middle of the road, after you angrily chased him all the way across town, knocked him down, and drove your car over him twice, you murdered him.

Likewise, if you inform a bank teller you will detonate a bomb if she doesn't give you all her cash, and then you walk out of the building with a sack full of currency, you will be guilty of stealing.

Adultery isn't a word found in our daily vocabulary. We're pretty sure it has something to do with sex but are totally confused as to what's right and what's wrong. *Encyclopedia Britannica* gives this definition: "sexual relations between a married person and someone other than the spouse," and adds that the term is "part of the marriage code of virtually every society."[10] Jesus used this word at least once in His sermons, so our study of **Matthew** will shed some light on exactly how God defines adultery. Stay tuned!

Exodus 20:17 and **Deuteronomy 5:21** (Beck). *"Do not covet your neighbor's wife."*

"Covet" is another word we don't use often today. This commandment deals with thoughts rather than actions—issues like greed and desiring something that's not available because it belongs to someone else.

Here, then, are gleanings of the edicts relating to sex in the codebook of the Old Testament:

THE FIRSTBORN

Exodus 13:1–2 (Beck). *The LORD spoke to Moses: "Set aside as holy every firstborn of any mother in Israel, among both people and animals; they are Mine."*

Exodus 13:11–13 (Beck). *"When the LORD brings you to the land of the Canaanites . . . give the LORD every firstborn, also every firstborn of your animals; if they are males, they belong to the LORD. Redeem every firstborn donkey with an animal from the flock, and if you don't redeem it, break its neck. And redeem every firstborn of your children."*

That first generation, at Mount Sinai, would have vividly remembered the grief and anger of the Egyptians as every family that wasn't covered by the blood of a Passover lamb discovered the sudden deaths in their household. To be sure, the Israelites would always remember that they had been spared from that plague; the first child born of every woman was to be redeemed with a special sacrificial offering.

CALL FOR ABSTINENCE

Exodus 19:1–15 (Beck). Shortly after crossing the Red Sea, the Israelites reached Mount Sinai. God was about to give His people His set of instructions for living—the owners' manuals, as it were, for the bodies we inhabit. In preparation, Moses told the people to wash their clothes and *"Be ready for the day after tomorrow . . . Don't go near a woman."*

Their focus for those three days was to be anticipation for actually hearing words from God. Having intercourse during that time would have been a distraction.

FEMALE HEBREW SLAVES

Exodus 21:7–11 (Beck). *"When a man sells his daughter to be a concubine, she should not go free"* [at the end of seven years] *"the way male slaves do. If her master decides not to make her his wife, because he doesn't like her, he can let her go for a price, but he has no right to sell her to outsiders, since he has cheated her. If he makes her his son's wife, he must treat her like a daughter. If he marries another, he cannot deprive her of food, clothing, or intercourse. If he doesn't do these three things for her, she should go free without anyone paying anything."*

Thus, if a Hebrew man purchased a Hebrew woman as a concubine, either for himself or for his son, then changed his mind, her father could buy her back. If the man decided to simply take an additional wife, he was stuck with this one, in that position, for the rest of her life. Should he neglect her in any way, she would be free to leave him.

Hebrew slaves, male or female, were to be treated as indentured servants, not as property. Even in a concubine relationship, women had guaranteed rights.

INJURY TO A PREGNANT WOMAN

Exodus 21:22 (Beck). "*If men who are fighting hit a pregnant woman so that she delivers her child prematurely but there is no harm to either mother or child, the man should pay the fine her husband puts on him.*"

To cause a premature birth, even if done accidentally, was punishable by fine. God values human life at all ages.

RAPE

Rape and seduction are covered in several passages.

Exodus 22:16–17. Seduction of an unengaged virgin meant marriage, complete with payment to the girl's father. Even if the father refused to allow his daughter to marry the man, the fine still had to be paid.

Leviticus 19:20–22. If a slave who was engaged was raped, the woman belonged to whoever owned her as a slave. She also belonged, almost but not quite, to the man she was to marry. The rapist had to bring a sacrifice to pay for his action. They both narrowly escaped the death penalty but were punished, probably by whipping. We aren't told whether or not the woman obtained her freedom or was able to marry her fiancé (if indeed that was still a viable option).

Deuteronomy 22:23–24 (Beck). If an engaged woman was raped in a city, both of them were to be stoned to death, "*the girl because she didn't cry out, being in the town, and the man because he sexually violated another man's wife; and so you must get rid of such wickedness among you.*"

Remember, they were in tents in Moses' time, and later on, in walled cities. People lived close to each other—more like today's apartments than in separate houses. Thus, someone should have been close enough to hear the woman scream and to have captured or chased off the perpetrator.

Unfortunately, women today don't have that kind of available protection.

Deuteronomy 22:25–27 (Beck). If an engaged woman was raped out in the open countryside, *"then only the man who lay with her must die. Don't do anything to the girl; there's no sin for which the girl deserves to die . . . the engaged girl cried out, but there was nobody to save her."*

The perpetrator received a death sentence. The woman was not punished. It wasn't her fault.

Deuteronomy 22:28–29. If a man raped a woman who wasn't engaged, he would discover that he was now married to her, owed her father the standard bride price, and was not allowed to ever divorce her.

No matter how much a man's hormones rage, there is no such thing, in God's eyes, as unintentional intercourse. There is always a decision, on the part of one or the other individual, not to stop the process. *"One flesh,"* after all, was part of the original definition of marriage (**Genesis 2:24).**

The mind and spirit are supposed to be in control of the body.

BESTIALITY

Exodus 22:19 (Beck). *"Anyone who has intercourse with an animal must be killed."*

Leviticus 18:23 (Beck) adds that *"it is perversion"* while **Leviticus 20:15–16** (Beck) declares *"they must be killed,"* along with instructions to kill the animal. **Deuteronomy 27:21** (Beck), which is part of the blessings and cursings that are to be proclaimed in the Promised Land, repeats the message: *"A curse on anyone who lies with any animal."*

MEDICAL ISSUES

Blood is one of the important themes of Scripture. Except for those who experience frequent nosebleeds, the sexual part of a woman's body does more bleeding than the entire rest of her anatomy, put together. Therefore, for her, blood is definitely relevant to the topic of sex.

Leviticus 17:11 (Beck). "*A body's life is in the blood, and I direct you to put it on the altar to atone for your lives, because it is the blood that atones for a life.*"

The very first sin, in the garden of Eden, was covered by the blood sacrifice of animals that were killed to provide clothing for Adam and Eve. Likewise, Cain's sacrifice was rejected while Abel's was approved because only Abel presented a blood sacrifice. Ultimately, however, the blood of animals—although it reminded worshipers that it should have been their blood, their death as payment for their errors—could not wipe their sins out of God's book of remembrance. Only God, the promised Messiah, by shedding His blood on the cross, would be able to take their punishment, pay their fines, and save them from eternal death.

CHILDBIRTH

The birth of a baby involves a great deal of blood. Therefore, childbirth has special regulations:

Leviticus 12:1–5 (Beck). God decreed, "*When a woman gives birth and has a boy, she is unclean for seven days, the same number of days she is unclean during her menstruation. But on the eighth day he should be circumcised. And for thirty-three days she should stay home because she must be cleansed from her bleeding and not touch anything holy or go into the holy place till the time the cleansing from her bleeding is over.*" If she has a girl, both time frames are doubled.

In a nutshell, if the baby was a boy, the mother was required to remain at that location for seven days. On the eighth day, the boy was to be circumcised, which identified him as an Israelite (one of God's people), and she was given a bit more freedom of movement, although she was not allowed to touch anything pertaining to the tabernacle (later synagogue or temple) for another thirty-three days, for a total of forty days under restrictions. If the infant was a girl, since there was no rite of circumcision to mark her as part of God's family, the time intervals became two weeks in quarantine and sixty-six days more before she could enter God's house.

Leviticus 12:6–8 (Beck). When that time was complete, "*She should bring to the priest . . . a yearling lamb for a burnt offering, and a young pigeon or a turtledove to be sacrificed for sin . . . Then she will be clean from her flow of blood . . . If she is too poor to give a lamb, she should take two turtledoves or two young pigeons, one for a burnt offering and the other to be sacrificed for sin.*"

Finally, when the baby boy was forty days old, or eighty days after the birth of a baby girl, the mother was required to take a ritual bath. Then she and her child were welcome to approach the tabernacle.

This passage has an impact on the timing of what is normally called "The Christmas Story." When Baby Jesus was presented in the temple forty days after Christmas Eve, Mary and Joseph were still classified as poor people, since for their sacrificial offering they brought birds, not a lamb. Therefore, the Wise Men had definitely not yet arrived.

OTHER BODILY FLUIDS

Bodily fluids can carry diseases. That is why in our day doctors, nurses, and even dentists wear gloves when treating patients. The gloves protect the health care professional from being attacked by any germs that might be lurking, plus, they avoid spreading diseases from patient to patient.

Not only were surgical gloves unavailable, but the Israelites also didn't have a disinfectant dispenser at the entrance to every tent. These special precautions were needed for those reasons, but these rules also ensured an attitude of respect, both for themselves and for those who needed to be in their vicinity. Ultimately, an attempt to be clean also exhibits a respect for God.

Remember, too, there were times during those forty years in the wilderness when the people panicked because there wasn't enough water to drink, let alone to keep their bodies clean. Even after they settled in the Promised Land, there were years of drought so severe that all the streams dried up. In both of those conditions, isolation at least kept potential problems segregated.

Gentlemen got their instructions first:

Leviticus 15:1-15 (Beck). This time God told both Moses and Aaron, *"When a man has a discharge from his body, his discharge is unclean . . . whether it flows from his body or is stopped, he is still unclean . . ."* Literally, everything that man touches needs to be laundered. Anyone who touches the things he has touched *". . . should wash his clothes, bathe in water, and be unclean till evening."* The only exception seems to be that if the man washed his hands before he touched the item, then the second person is released from that regulation. Even pottery had to be smashed. God definitely did not want people spreading germs.

"When the person with the discharge is getting cleansed from it, he should add seven days for his cleansing and wash his clothes and bathe in fresh water; then he's clean. On the eighth day he should take two turtledoves or two young pigeons and come before the LORD at the entrance of the tent where He meets with you and give them to the priest . . . so the priest will atone for him before the LORD for his discharge."

That would seem to cover the situation in cases of illness or the ravages of old age.

Leviticus 15:16-17 (Beck). *"When a man has an emission of semen, he should bathe his whole body in water and be unclean till evening. Any garment and any leather with semen on it should be washed in water and be unclean till evening."*

This, then, applied to more normal times.

Deuteronomy 23:9–11 (Beck). *"When you're out in a camp going against your enemies, keep yourselves from anything foul. If there's anyone among you who gets unclean by an emission at night, he should go outside the camp and not come into the camp. When evening comes, he should wash, and when the sun goes down, he may come into the camp."*

Even in times of war, rules of cleanliness were to be observed.

Now it's the women's turn, with the common problem listed first:

Leviticus 15:19–24 (Beck). *"When a woman has her regular flow of blood from her body, she goes on being unclean seven days."* Anyone or anything she touched was to be considered unclean. And anyone who touched anything she had touched would also be required to *"wash his clothes, bathe in water, and be unclean till evening."* In addition, *"If a man lies with her and some of her menstruation comes on him, he is unclean seven days, and any bed he lies on is unclean."*

Considering how profusely some women bleed at the time of their monthly period, the idea that any item under her would need to be laundered afterward is quite understandable, especially since at that time in history, they didn't have all the feminine hygiene items available today. Since some women experience very few problems while others are absolutely miserable, a full week's break from normal activities, including a ban on intercourse if she were married, would have been quite welcome. Then when her week was ended, she got to take a bath and feel like a human being again. Israelite communities often had a separate swimming pool/ritual bathing area for just that purpose.

Leviticus 15:25–30. All other female blood flows were to be treated the same as a menstrual period, with all the same restrictions and cleansing requirements. In those cases, on the eighth day after the flow stopped, she was to offer two turtledoves or two pigeons. Nothing is said about a bath, but I'm sure she would have wanted one. That would be the rule for a woman with a more serious problem.

Some regulations applied to both partners regarding intercourse:

Leviticus 15:18 (Beck). *"When a man has sex relations with a woman with an emission of semen, they should bathe in water and be unclean till evening."*

Leviticus 20:18 (Beck). *"When a man lies with a woman while she is menstruating and has intercourse with her, he lays bare her source, and she has uncovered the source of her blood; both must be cut off from their people."*

Therefore, for seven days each month, intercourse was off-limits. The injunction also appears in **Leviticus 18:19.**

Leviticus 15:31–33 (Beck). To summarize the subject of bodily fluids, *"Warn the Israelites about their uncleanness, or they will die from it by making My tabernacle among them unclean.*

"That is the law for one who has a discharge or a flow of semen to make him unclean, for her who is unclean from menstruation, for anyone, man or woman, having a flow, and for a man who lies with a woman when she's unclean."

In a nutshell, God has reasons for those restrictions.

INCEST

Incest is a topic mentioned at least eight times in the instructions Moses delivered from God. You'll find them especially in **Leviticus 18** and **20** and **Deuteronomy 22** and **27**. The first mention gives the reason. Following that is a long listing of prohibited sexual unions.

Leviticus 18:6 (Beck). *"Don't have sex relations with anyone related to you by blood; I am the LORD."*

That list of forbidden unions (all quoted from Beck) includes:

- Your mother
- Your father's wife (*"Both must be killed because they deserve to die."*)
- Your son's or daughter's daughter
- Your father's or mother's sister

- Your brother's wife*
- Both a woman and her daughter (*"It is a shameful wrong. The man and the two women must be burned to get rid of a shameful wrong among you."*)
- Both a woman and her granddaughter (this, too, is *"a shameful wrong"*)
- Sisters, as long as both are alive
- Your daughter-in-law (*"Both must be killed; they have done a perverted thing; they deserve to die."*)
- Your sister, your half-sister, or your step-sister (*"It is a shameful thing, and they must be cut off before the eyes of the people. He has had intercourse with his sister and deserves to be punished."*)
- Your uncle's wife (*"They deserve to be punished and must die without children."*)
- Your mother-in-law (if you do, you are under *a curse*)

* In the case of the brother's wife, this restriction would only be true while the brother was still alive. Once the brother died, the following applied:

Deuteronomy 25:5–10 (Beck). *"When brothers live together and one of them dies without a child, his widow should not go outside the family and marry a stranger. Her husband's brother should marry her, have sex relations with her, and so do his duty as her husband's brother. Then the first son she has should count as the dead brother's son . . ."*

If the brother says he doesn't want to do that, then the woman should report him to the city rulers. But if he still refuses to take her, *". . . his brother's widow should go up to him while the elders are watching, take his shoe off his foot, spit in his face, and declare, 'That's what is done to a man who doesn't build his brother's family.'"*

For an illustration of an application of this rule, see the account of **Ruth**.

So how did Abraham get by with marrying his half-sister? For that matter, the children of Adam and Eve married their brothers and sisters. Noah's grandchildren married cousins or siblings.

It is quite probable that the number of mutations in the human genetic code (errors in our DNA) were fairly minor, even in the days of the patriarchs, for in the original creation, the entire bodies of Adam and Eve were perfect. By the time of Moses, 400 years after Abraham, the results of family in-breeding—a practice common among royalty in Egypt—could have revealed some fairly serious problems.

SOMEONE ELSE'S WIFE

Another subject mentioned in many places in the Bible is the situation when one sexual partner is already married to someone else. The circumstances are always stated in terms of someone and his neighbor's wife.

I suspect one reason the man was assumed to be the instigator was for the protection of any children who might be born of that union. After all, the biological mother of a child is usually fairly easy to identify, at least immediately following the birth. Biological fathers could seem to be anonymous, thus leaving some other man responsible for raising a child that is not his own.

The bottom line here is, if a woman is married, she is off-limits for everybody else.

The strongest statements are these:

Leviticus 20:10 (Beck). *"When anyone has sex relations with another man's wife, with his neighbor's wife, both must be killed for their adultery."*

Deuteronomy 22:22 (Beck). *"If a man is caught having intercourse with a married woman, both of them, the man who lay with the woman and the woman, must die, and so you must get rid of such wickedness in Israel."*

Affairs are not acceptable.

CHILD SACRIFICE

Leviticus 18:21 (Beck). *"Don't give Molech any of your children by burning them alive—don't defile the name of your God; I am the LORD."*

Molech was an idol[11] that was worshiped by sacrificing young children. Somehow that doesn't seem much different from aborting babies.

Leviticus 20:1–5 (Beck). *"If any Israelite or any stranger who lives in Israel gives any of his children to Molech, he must be killed. The people of the land must stone him. I will oppose that man and cut him off from his people for giving some of his children to Molech, making my holy place unclean and my holy name unholy. If the people of the country shut their eyes to a person who gives some of his children to Molech and don't kill him, I will oppose that man and his family; I will cut him off from his people, and all who go after him lusting after Molech."*

Thus, if a person sacrificed a child to the fires of that idol, if the people around that area didn't penalize them for doing so, the entire community would be punished. God takes the lives of children very seriously.

HOMOSEXUALITY

Leviticus 18:22 (Beck). *"Don't lie with a man as with a woman; it is abominable."*

Leviticus 20:13 (Beck). *"When a man lies with another man as with a woman, both do something abominable and must be killed; they deserve to die."*

Remember what the Lord did to Sodom!

PROSTITUTION

Leviticus 19:29 (Beck). *"Don't make your daughter unholy by making her a prostitute, or the country will turn to prostitution and be full of vice."*

Deuteronomy 23:17–18 (Beck). *"No woman in Israel should become a temple prostitute, and no man in Israel should become a temple prostitute. The money paid to a female prostitute or a male prostitute should not be brought into the house of the LORD your God to keep a vow, because the LORD your God abhors both of them."*

The practice of cult prostitution, both male and female, was part of many pagan worship rituals. Thus, God found them objectionable on more than one count.

RULES FOR PRIESTS

The next several rules applied only to priests:

Leviticus 21:7 (Beck). Priests were not allowed to marry prostitutes, divorcees, or women who had been raped, *"because a priest is God's holy man."*

Leviticus 21:9 (Beck). If a priest's daughter *"makes herself unholy by being a prostitute, she makes her father unholy. She must be burned."*

Leviticus 21:13–15 (Beck). Of the high priest, God decreed, *"He must marry a virgin. He must not marry a widow, divorced woman, fallen woman, or prostitute, but a virgin of his own people to avoid making his children unholy among his people, because I the LORD make him holy."*

The high priesthood was supposed to be a hereditary office, so anyone potentially eligible would need to marry accordingly.

Leviticus 21:17–20 (Beck). A priest with physical problems was not to be allowed to approach the altar to offer sacrifices. *"No one should come* *near who has a defect, who is blind or lame, no one with a mutilated face or a limb too long, with a broken foot or hand, no hunchback, no dwarf, no one with a disease of his eyes, with any skin diseases, no one with crushed testicles."*

God makes it very clear that priests are to follow a stricter set of rules than what is acceptable for the general public, for the priest represents God to the people.

Leviticus 22:4–7 (Beck). *"No descendant of Aaron who is a leper or has a discharge should eat any of the holy gifts till he is clean. If you touch anyone unclean by contact with the dead or you have an emission of semen, or you touch any reptile that makes you unclean or a human being whatever way he may be unclean—if you touch them, you will be unclean till evening and must not eat any of the holy things unless you have bathed your body in water. When the sun goes down, you're clean, and then you may eat the holy gifts because they are your food."*

Thus, restrictions for priests were not just related to sex. Any means whereby germs could be transmitted would require temporary quarantine.

JEALOUS ACCUSATION

If a jealous husband existed in the tribes of Israel, God had designed a means to settle the dispute:

Numbers 5:12–31 (Beck). *"If any man's wife goes wrong and is unfaithful to him and another man has intercourse with her without her husband knowing it and she has become unclean but keeps it secret, not having been caught in the act and there being no witness to accuse her, if then a jealous spirit comes over him and makes him jealous over his wife . . ."* then he was to bring her to the priest, along with a specified offering.

The priest was then supposed to sprinkle some dust from the floor of the sanctuary into clean water, add ink from a written copy of the accusation, and the woman had to drink that concoction. If she became sick, the water would make her *"thigh waste away"* and her *"belly swell"* and she was guilty. If the woman did not experience these problems, then her husband had been wrong in his suspicions.

VOWS

Numbers 30:1–15. If someone made a solemn vow to do something, the Lord made a distinction between men and women:

- If a man made a vow, no matter what, he was stuck with it.
- If a woman, still living in her home of origin, made a vow . . .
  - If her father immediately told her she couldn't do that, then she was excused from the vow, and the Lord promised to forgive her for not carrying through with her pledge.
  - If her father heard about it but said nothing, then her vow remained.
- If a woman got married while she was under a vow . . .
  - If her husband opposed her the moment he heard about it, she was excused from that vow, and the Lord promised to forgive her.
  - If her husband heard but said nothing, her vow remained and possibly became his responsibility.
- If a woman was widowed or divorced, her vows remained valid.

PORNOGRAPHY

Pornography was a major part of idol worship. As they neared the Promised Land, some warnings and directions were in order:

Deuteronomy 7:25 (Beck). *"Burn the images of their gods without hankering for the silver and gold on them or taking it for yourself, or it will trap you, because it is abominable to the LORD your God."*

Thus, of the pornographic statues left behind by the people who lived in the Promised Land, they were not to even try to save the gold or silver—just burn (or smash and melt) everything.

Deuteronomy 12:2–4 (Beck). *"Completely destroy all the places where the people you're driving out served their gods . . . Tear down their altars, smash their pillars, burn their sacred Asherah posts, cut down the images of their gods, and wipe out their names from their places. Don't do what they do when you worship the LORD your God."*

Again, they were to get rid of the pornography and all the locations used for cult prostitution, both male and female.

Deuteronomy 16:21–22 (Beck). *"Don't set up any wooden post as a sacred pole for Asherah beside the altar of the LORD your God that you make, and don't set up any holy stone pillar; these are things the LORD your God hates."*

After they removed the detestable idols, they weren't supposed to reconstruct them all over again.

MILITARY RULES

There were also some interesting regulations for wartime. First, before calling up troops for battle, the commander was required to ask:

Deuteronomy 20:7 (Beck). *"Has anyone become engaged to a woman and not married her? Go back home, or you may die in battle and someone else will marry her."*

Deuteronomy 21:10–14 (Beck). If a soldier brought home a war bride, taken from among the captives, she must shave off all her hair, trim her nails, and discard the clothes she came with in exchange for an outfit appropriate for an Israelite woman. She was to be given a full month to mourn for her parents, after which she could get married to the soldier. If within those thirty days the soldier decided he didn't *"like her any more,"* she was free to go wherever she wanted. In no case could the soldier sell her or treat her as a slave, for he had *"sexually humbled her."*

Deuteronomy 24:5 (Beck). *"When a man is just married, he shouldn't go out with the army or get any special duty. For one year he should be free at home to make the woman he married happy."*

Modern military families would really appreciate this regulation.

MULTIPLE WIVES

Deuteronomy 21:15–17 (Beck). *"If a man has two wives and loves the one and not the other, and both have children, but the unloved wife has the first son, when he gives what he has to his sons as their inheritance, he can't make the son of the wife he loves the firstborn, setting aside the unloved wife's son who is the firstborn, but he must recognize the unloved wife's son as the first-born and give him a double share of everything he owns, because he is the first child of his vigor and has the right of the firstborn."*

When we remember all the problems with Jacob's dysfunctional family, we realize this codified fair treatment.

CLOTHING

Deuteronomy 22:5 (Beck). *"A woman shouldn't wear a man's things, and a man shouldn't wear a woman's clothes, because the LORD your God is disgusted with anyone who does these things."*

We can only guess at the difference between Hebrew men's and women's clothing in the time of Moses. We all have mental images of pictures, perhaps even movies, depicting that era. But we don't actually know what they wore. Any of the artwork on which we would base our judgment would have been created hundreds or even thousands of years after the fact. Part of the Law given at Mount Sinai prohibited making graven images, so there are no Hebrew statues of that period. There are statues and carvings that depict other peoples of that era, but even if any Egyptian monuments would depict the Hebrews as slaves, we would not anticipate a true indication of styles, for slaves typically aren't able to set their own dress code.

While we do have names for some of the garments, that still doesn't give us the whole picture. Just within the time frame of U.S. history, a skirt could require hoops, a bustle, or several can cans. It could sweep the floor or be a mini that barely covered the subject. Fashions change, often drastically. Therefore, we don't actually know how different "different" is supposed to be.

There is, however, a modern practice called "cross-dressing" that would definitely seem to be covered by this passage.

PROOF OF VIRGINITY

Deuteronomy 22:13–15 (Beck). *"If a man marries a woman and has intercourse with her and then hates her, accuses her of things he's made up, and gives her a bad name by saying, 'I married this woman, but when I came to her, I found she wasn't a virgin,' then the girl's father and mother should take the evidence of her being a virgin and bring it to the elders of the town at the gate."*

If, indeed, a woman was a virgin on her wedding night, she would have bled, at least a little, at the time of penetration. Therefore, the sheet or outfit on which the couple had intercourse would have had blood spots. Apparently, that cloth became the property of the girl's father for him to keep as evidence. In fact, I wonder if perhaps the newlyweds signed and maybe even dated the fabric, turning it into an easily identified legal document.

Deuteronomy 22:16–17 (Beck). *"The girl's father should tell the elders, 'I gave this man my daughter to be his wife, but he hates her and now accuses her of things he's made up, saying, 'I found your daughter wasn't a virgin.' But here is the proof that my daughter was a virgin.'—and they should spread out the garment before the elders of the town."*

That cloth, therefore, would be all the evidence the court of law needed in order to declare the girl innocent.

Deuteronomy 22:18–19 (Beck). *"Then the elders of that town should take the man and punish him and fine him a hundred shekels of silver, giving it to the girl's father, because the husband gave a virgin in Israel a bad name. She will be his wife, and he can't divorce her as long as he lives."*

This accusation was not to be done lightly. If evidence proved innocence, the husband was to be publicly humiliated and fined, plus he was stuck with her as his wife. In fact, this probably falls under the rule that her food, her clothing allowance, and their times of intercourse were not allowed to diminish.

Deuteronomy 22:20–21 (Beck). *"But if the claim is true and there was no proof the girl was a virgin, take the girl to the door of her father's home, and the men of her town should stone her to death because she has done a disgraceful thing in Israel by sinning sexually in her father's home. And so you must get rid of such wickedness among you."*

This was the dilemma Joseph faced. Mary was still a virgin. They had not had intercourse because they were only engaged, not married. Therefore, there was no *evidence of virginity* (ESV) for her father to present to the judges. And yet, she was pregnant, which to logical minds said she couldn't possibly still be a virgin—until an angel invaded Joseph's life . . .

CASTRATION

Deuteronomy 23:1 (Beck). *"If anyone's testicles are crushed or his sex organ is cut off, he should not come into the LORD's congregation."* That would seem to rule out gender reassignment surgery. Eunuchs were not allowed in tabernacle or temple.

ENVIRONMENTAL CLEANLINESS

Deuteronomy 23:12–14 (Beck). *"You should have a special place outside the camp where you can go. Carry a spade with your tools, and when you're going to sit down out there, dig a hole with it, sit down, and then cover what you leave. The LORD your God moves around in your camp to save you and put your enemies at your mercy, and so your camp should be holy that he may see nothing indecent among you and turn away from you."*

They didn't have port-a-potties. That, however, was no excuse to expose the rest of the army, or the general population, to bodily wastes. Keeping their campsites clean because God walked among them also protected them from a host of diseases.

DIVORCE

This book stops with Song of Solomon. Lord willing, I do intend to write a second volume, covering the remainder of the Bible. The New Testament portions of this section concerning the Bible's words about divorce are drawn from the pages of that second volume.

Divorce wasn't in God's original formula for this world. Neither was death. But since we are no longer the perfect individuals that Adam and Eve were before Satan got his fangs into the human race, the subject of divorce was something Jesus needed to clarify in His teaching of the multitudes. He included it in His Sermon on the Mount. The Pharisees, always looking for a way to trip Him, brought up the issue again on at least one other occasion and received an even longer answer. Let's put all four of those sections together and analyze what God has to say about divorce.

Matthew 5:31–32 (Beck). *"It was said: 'Anyone who divorces his wife must give her a divorce paper.' But I tell you, anyone who divorces his wife, except for her being sexually unfaithful, makes her a partner in adultery. And also the man who marries the divorced woman is living in adultery."*

Mark 10:2–12 (Beck). *Some Pharisees came to Him. "Is it right for a man to divorce his wife?" they asked Him in order to test Him.*

"What did Moses order you to do?" He asked them.

"Moses let a man make out a divorce paper and divorce his wife," they said.

"He wrote this law for you on account of your closed minds," Jesus told them. "But when God made the world, He in the beginning made them a male and a female. That's why a man will leave his father and mother and the two will be one flesh. And so they are no more two but one flesh. Now, what God has joined together man must not separate."

In the house the disciples also asked Him about this. "If anyone divorces his wife," He answered them, "and marries another, he's living in adultery with her. And if a wife divorces her husband and marries another man, she's living in adultery."

Matthew 19:3–9 (Beck). *Some Pharisees, coming to Him to test Him, asked Him, "Is it right for a man to divorce his wife for any reason?"*

"Haven't you read," He asked them, "He who created them from the beginning made them a male and a female?" And He added: "That is why a man will leave his father and mother and live with his wife, and the two will be one flesh. And so they are no more two but one flesh. Now, what God has joined together man must not separate."

"Why, then, did Moses order a man to make out a divorce paper and divorce his wife?" they asked Him.

He answered them, "Because your minds are closed, Moses let you divorce your wives, but originally there was no such thing. I tell you, if anyone divorces his wife, except for adultery, and marries another, he's living in adultery."

Luke 16:18 (Beck). *"Anyone who divorces his wife and marries another is living in adultery. And the man who marries a woman divorced from her husband is living in adultery."*

Note that, in His rebuttal of the religious leaders, Jesus goes all the way back to creation for His answer. *"He who created them from the beginning made them a male and a female."* This pronouncement is, therefore, not just for the descendants of Abraham—it's for the descendants of Adam, which includes everybody. There are only two types of humans: XY and XX. And marriage is to be one of each, not one man and several wives, or one woman and several husbands.

The Bible also makes it clear that, as we will find in **Malachi 2:16** (Beck), God hates divorce.[12] Also, *"What therefore God has joined together, man must not separate,"* as both **Matthew** and **Mark** informed us.

But in a fallen world, perhaps as much for health and safety as for any other reason, God allows an exception. The operative term, in both **Matthew** passages, is *porneia*. It's the Greek base from which we get our word "pornography."[13] Various English translations use *adultery, sexual unfaithfulness, fornication, sexual immorality, sexual promiscuity, unchastity,* or *infidelity* when translating it here. A complete overview of the meaning of *porneia* can be found in *Theological Dictionary of the New Testament.*[14]

Thus, if a spouse is practicing a lifestyle that embraces an extra-marital affair or is selling or renting his or her own or another's body for the purpose of sex, in those cases, God allows His children a way out of a bad situation.

As I understand these passages, if A marries B, and sometime later, it is discovered that B is practising *porneia*, then A has God's permission to file for a divorce. A is not required to do so, although, in today's culture, divorce is often necessary to provide a legal structure for custody and support of any children who may be involved. Since, by this point, the error is one of lifestyle rather than a single infraction, while A is required to forgive B (as we are reminded in the Lord's Prayer), A is not required to trust B or to welcome him or her back to home and bed.

This is where the subject of divorce ties into our study. In fact, this is the Old Testament section about which the Pharisees were trying to trip Jesus.

Deuteronomy 24:1–4 (Beck). If a man *"finds something offensive about"* his wife, and then gives her *"a divorce paper"* and tosses her out of his house, then if she marries someone else, who either dies or also divorces her, the original husband *is not allowed to marry her again. "The LORD would abhor that. Don't bring guilt on the land the LORD your God is giving you as your own."*

Following the divorce, anyone who B might marry would also be branded with B's *porneia* status. A, however, might have God's permission to marry someone new. As we see here, once B does get married and then is either divorced again or his or her new spouse dies, that person is never allowed to remarry A. God defines that as "national pollution."

In chapter six, we will discover that, in the days of **Ezra** and **Nehemiah,** God actually required some divorces because the non-Jewish wives were practicing the idolatrous actions of the nations from which they had come, and therefore, in order to remove that temptation from returning Jews, divorce was the lesser of two evils.

St. Paul discusses another facet of this issue in **1 Corinthians 7** (Beck), the situation where the husband or wife either deserts the other or tosses them out. Apparently, in the time of the early church, when people became Christian, some thought they could no longer live with their unbelieving spouse. Paul assures his readers that leaving their spouse is definitely not required. In fact, he advises believers to stay married, if possible, as a witness to their family. However, *if the unbelieving person leaves, let him go.* Short of some kind of confinement, you really can't force someone to stay married if he or she is determined not to be.

Porneia breaks marriages apart. So does desertion. Broken marriages pave the way for broken societies. Even extended families and casual friendships are affected by a couple's divorce, no matter what the reason.

The ones who are most damaged in that family division are the children; they often believe the situation is all their fault. They could easily think that their identity has been blown to smithereens—in fact, that they should have never existed in the first place.

If you are that child, I assure you that you are not a mistake. No matter what the circumstances of your birth, the Creator of the universe wanted this world to include the particular combination of DNA that is uniquely you. He has a niche that needs your talents, a project He wants you to complete, a spot where you can serve Him. He could have moved heaven and earth so that, on the day you were conceived, your parents would have been in different cities, different states, perhaps even different countries, to prevent your conception. They may have had other children later, but none of them would have been *you*. He *could* have done that, but He didn't. To Him, you're special.

No matter what your parents or you or your siblings have done; no matter that your parents can't seem to get along now; no matter that the court says you have to be bounced back and forth like a ball in a tennis match—there is one constant you can always hold on to. God loves you. He made you. He could read the coding of your very first cell and see who you would be today. And He wants you to trust Him—with your present circumstances and your eternal destiny.

FIGHT FAIR

Deuteronomy 25:11–12 (Beck). If two Israelites are fighting, *"and the wife of one comes to rescue her husband from the other who is striking him and she reaches out and takes hold of his sex organs, cut off her hand without any pity."*

DAUGHTERS OF ZELOPHEHAD

It was time to discuss the division of the Promised Land. God had told Moses that he would not be able to cross the Jordan River and enter Canaan, but that didn't keep him from taking care of some final details, including directions for how the area should be split.

Numbers 27:1-11 and **36:1-12.** The five daughters of Zelophehad, descendants of Joseph, requested a special ruling from Moses. The land was to be divided by tribe, then clan and family, and apportioned to the men, through whom both name and real estate would be inherited (much like our American surnames passing from father to son). But Zelophehad had no sons, only five daughters.

God decreed that the girls should, in that case, be allowed to inherit. To keep their areas as a part of their designated tribe, however, the ladies would be required to marry cousins. Thus, in an era when women were often not allowed to own property, God overruled common custom so that justice was served.

REASONS AND CONSEQUENCES

With all these rules and regulations, some may wonder if God is trying to take all the fun out of life. **Exodus 34, Leviticus 18 and 20, and Deuteronomy 7, 9,** and **28,** give us God's attitude toward ignoring His rules regarding sex but also dealing with a host of other issues. He also includes instructions for how His people were to deal with idols, which were pornographic in many cases, and the people who worshiped them, often by cult prostitution, in the land they were about to enter.

While I urge you to do further research into those six chapters, here are the major points:

Leviticus 18:24–28 (Beck). *"Don't make yourselves unclean in any of these ways, because by these practices all the people made themselves unclean whom I'm driving out ahead of you; and so the land became unclean; I'm punishing it for its wrongs, and the land is vomiting up those who live in it. Keep My rules and My laws, and don't any of you, Israelites or strangers living among you, do any of these abominable things. The people of the land who were there before you did all these abominable things, and so the land became unclean. The land will vomit you up too, if you make it unclean, as it vomited up the people who were there before you."*

The preceding verses, especially **21–23**, describe activities that were being practiced by the people living in the land of Canaan (modern-day Israel). Those behaviors, apparently more than any other deeds, were the reason God told His people to totally wipe those natives off the face of the globe, not sparing men, women, or children, and in some cases, even killing all their livestock and burning their villages.

Leviticus 18:29–30 (Beck). *"If you do any of these abominable things, you will be cut off from your people. So keep My instructions, and don't practice any of the abominable things done before you came, and don't make yourselves unclean with them: I the LORD am your God."*

Even after the Israelites had wiped out the natives, they needed to be vigilant, for some of those artifacts or ideas might surface again. If such abominations showed up, they were to be dealt with speedily and thoroughly. Unfortunately, the Israelites never completely annihilated the idol-worshiping tribes, so the prohibited activities just kept coming back to haunt them.

Deuteronomy 9:4–5 (Beck). The Israelites weren't getting the Promised Land because they were the good guys, but rather, *"It is because these nations are wicked that the LORD is driving them out ahead of you. Not because you're righteousness or your heart is right are you going in to take their land, but because those people are wicked, the LORD your God is driving them out ahead of you, and because the LORD wants to keep His promise He made by an oath to your fathers Abraham, Isaac, and Jacob."*

God had promised the land to Abraham, Isaac, and Jacob. He would keep that promise. But the reason He was transferring ownership from Canaanites to Israelites at that point in history was that the nations that were living in the Promised Land needed to be wiped off the face of the earth, lest their wickedness, and probably even some of their diseases, spread.

Exodus 34:12–16 (Beck). *"Be careful not to make a treaty with anyone living in the land where you're going, or they'll be a trap among you. No, tear down their altars, smash their sacred pillars, and cut down their sacred poles of Asherah. Don't worship any other God, because the LORD is called the Jealous One—He is a jealous God. If you should dare to make a treaty with anyone living in the land, where they lust after their gods and sacrifice to their gods, they'll invite you, and you'll eat their sacrifices; and you'll have your sons marry their daughters, and when their daughters lust after their gods, they'll lead your sons to lust after them too."*

Thus, the rule would be to kill *all* the Canaanite inhabitants of the Promised Land or totally chase them out of the country. In addition, all the native peoples' worship items were to be totally destroyed. God wanted to remove every possible temptation for His people to stray from a true understanding and worship of Him. Unfortunately, they didn't follow directions any better than we do.

Deuteronomy 7:1–5 (Beck). *"When the LORD your God brings you to the land you're about to enter and take over and clears out of your way many nations . . . seven nations greater and stronger than you . . . then destroy them completely, and don't make a treaty with them or begin favoring them. Don't intermarry with them . . . because they will turn your sons away from Me to serve other gods. Then the LORD will get very angry with you and quickly destroy you . . . Tear down their altars, smash their pillars, cut down their sacred Asherah posts, and burn their idols."*

Killing the people, however, would not be sufficient to wipe out all their evil practices. The pornography they left behind must also be smashed and burned.

Deuteronomy 28:58–68 (Beck). In summary, God warns, *"If you are not careful to do everything in this law, everything written in this book, and to fear this wonderful and awesome name THE LORD YOUR GOD, the LORD will bring extraordinary plagues on you and your descendants, great and continual plagues and severe diseases lasting a long time. He will bring back on you every disease of the Egyptians that you dread, and they will cling to you. The LORD will bring on you also every kind of sickness and plague not written in this book of the law till you're wiped out. There will be only a few left . . . because you didn't obey the LORD your God. Just as the LORD once delighted in making you a happy and large people, so the LORD will delight in destroying and wiping you out, and you will be torn from the land you're about to enter and take over. And the LORD will scatter you among all the people from one end of the world to the other . . . You will live in terror day and night, and you'll never feel sure of your life.*

IDOL WORSHIP

An incident near the end of their forty-year desert wandering illustrated exactly what the Lord had warned them about. You may remember Balaam's donkey—the one that talked. This is actually the tail end of that story.

Numbers 25:1–5 (Beck). Perched on the edge of the Promised Land, *the people started sinning sexually with Moab's women, who invited the people to the sacrifices to their gods, where the people ate as they worshiped their gods. As the Israelites paired off for the worship of the Baal at Peor, the LORD got very angry with Israel. "Take all the leaders of the people," the LORD told Moses, "and hang them up in the light of the sun for the LORD, to turn the LORD's fierce anger away from Israel." So Moses told the judges of Israel, "Each of you, kill those of your men who have paired themselves off for the Baal at Peor."*

The Moabite women eagerly introduced the Israelite men to the various practices of Baal worship. But it wasn't a game. The Berkeley translation of the Bible has this footnote at **Judges 6:26** regarding the shame images beside the altar of Baal: "A stump on each side of the Baal altar, one with the secret parts of a woman and the other of a man carved on it; by it the Baal worshippers committed lewdness in the name of religion. Temple prostitution was a sacred part of Baal ritual."[15] It was necessary to nip this in the bud and, in fact, to make an example of those who had fallen for that seduction.

Numbers 25:6–9 (Beck). *Just then one of the Israelites came and brought to his kinsmen a Midianite woman in plain view of Moses and the whole community of Israel . . . When Phinehas, the son of Eleazar, the son of Aaron the priest, saw it, he left the congregation and, taking a spear in his hand, went after the Israelite into the bedroom and drove the spear through both of them.*

The plague was stopped, but not until twenty-four thousand had died.

The Midianites (descendants of Abraham through the concubine he took after Sarah died) had joined forces with the Moabites by the start of **Numbers 22**. Moses' wife, Zipporah, was from the tribe of Midian, quite possibly from a family who still believed in the God of Abraham, but these Midianites were definitely idol worshipers.

Numbers 25:10–13. Because Phinehas had taken swift and decisive action, God promised that one of his descendants would always be a priest.

Numbers 25:17–18 (Beck). God's orders were clear. *"Attack the Midianites and defeat them because they attacked you with their vicious scheming."*

The ensuing battle killed *all their men* among that group of Midianites, including five kings, as per **Numbers 31:7–8** (Beck).

BLESSINGS FOR OBEDIENCE

There is a positive side to this picture. God also promises abundant blessings for faithfulness to His commands. He has designed those laws as a way to keep both our bodies and the relationships He has given us healthy.

Exodus 15:26 (Beck). Soon after they had crossed the Red Sea, God told them, *"If you will obey the LORD your God . . . and do what He says is right, listen to His orders, and keep all His laws, I will not have you suffer from any of the diseases I inflicted on Egypt, because I the LORD am He who heals you."*

This blessing certainly applied to sexually transmitted diseases and probably a host of other communicable maladies as well.

Deuteronomy 7:12–16 (Beck). God repeated that promise to the generation about to cross the Jordan: *"If you listen to these regulations and carefully do what they tell you, the LORD your God will keep His covenant and love for you as he swore to your fathers. He will love you and bless you and make you grow to be many . . . You will be more blessed than any other people. No one will be barren, male or female, among you or your cattle. The LORD will keep away from you every kind of sickness and put on you none of the ravaging Egyptian diseases you know but will inflict them on those who hate you. And you will consume all the people the LORD your God gives you; don't look kindly on them, and don't serve their gods, because they're a trap to you."*

This promise would be not just for the people, but their crops and livestock would benefit from the obedience of the citizens too.

In **Exodus, Leviticus, Numbers,** and **Deuteronomy,** we have discovered that idolatry and thus, pornography are a direct affront to God. Beyond that, and a multitude of rules and regulations on other subjects, when dealing with sex, most of the rest of the directives seem to fall into three categories:

- Blood, which is absolutely essential for physical life. When blood ceases to flow, an individual's life on this earth ends.
- Semen, which contains half the DNA needed to code a new individual. When timing, placement, and composition are in accord with God's blessing, life begins.
- Our body, which is *the earthly tent we live in* (**2 Corinthians 5:1**, Beck). Had St. Paul written that in this century, he might have

likened our bodies to spaceships *marvelously and wonderfully* constructed (**Psalm 139:14**, Beck).

Treat all three with respect. Respect yourself. Respect your family. Respect others around you. And, ultimately, respect God—the Giver of all three. He always knows what is best, for individuals as well as for nations.

3

BETWEEN MOSES
AND SAMUEL

AS **DEUTERONOMY** ENDED, Moses, then 120 years old, climbed alone to the top of Mount Nebo. From that vantage point, God showed him the entire Promised Land; then Moses died and God buried his body in a nearby valley (see **Deuteronomy 34** and **Jude 9**). In order to keep the people from making a shrine out of his grave, God completely disguised his burial spot.

RAHAB

Joshua 2:1. It was time for Joshua to take leadership of the tribes. His first action was to assign two young men to cross the Jordan River to scout out the walled city of Jericho and surrounding area. He sent them *secretly from Shittim as spies, saying, "Go, view the land, especially Jericho." And they went and came into the house of a prostitute whose name was Rahab and lodged there.*

We wonder at their choice, after all the warnings God had just given regarding forbidden women. Actually, though, approaching Rahab fit in perfectly with their undercover operation.

For one thing, their main quest wasn't to find out the geographical lay of the land. They might have been able to see the topography from the same mountains from which Moses had viewed the whole area. They were to infiltrate the enemy camp and discover the strengths and weaknesses of their opponents. Joshua had sent two young men, not just one, to keep each other out of trouble and thus, protect each other's backsides but also so that they could vouch for each other's actions when they returned to camp.

Given the descriptions God had already revealed about the general morality of the Canaanites, there were, no doubt, dozens of prostitutes who had set up shop in the metropolis of Jericho. For young men to visit such a place would have seemed, to the natives, only natural. Furthermore, for Rahab to close and lock her door in the middle of the day would have raised no eyebrows. And her rooms were apparently above most of the rest of the town, making it the perfect location from which to observe other residents.

Joshua 2:2–7. Rahab's neighbors had noticed the foreigners and reported them to the authorities. Realizing that her visitors belonged to the huge multitude encamped on the other side of the Jordan, and certain that the throng would be the winners in any armed conflict, Rahab chose to side with the Israelites. She hid the spies on her rooftop and lied to the officials who came to investigate. Then she disclosed to those scouts the terror felt by the inhabitants.

Joshua 2:8–11. *"I know that the LORD has given you the land, and that the fear of you has fallen upon us, and that all the inhabitants of the land melt away before you. For we have heard how the LORD dried up the water of the Red Sea before you when you came out of Egypt, and what you did to the two kings of the Amorites . . . And as soon as we heard it, our hearts melted, and there was no spirit left in any man because of you, for the LORD your God, he is God in the heavens above and on the earth beneath."*

Rahab believed that God was almighty. She, too, lived in terror of His judgment. She wanted out of her current situation, and these agents from His people were her only hope.

Joshua 2:12–13. *"Now then, please swear to me by the LORD that, as I have dealt kindly with you, you also will deal kindly with my father's house,* *and give me a sure sign that you will save alive my father and mother, my brothers and sisters, and all who belong to them."*

Rahab wasn't just worried about herself. She was concerned that her whole family would be annihilated when the battle arrived on their doorstep.

Joshua 2:14. The spies replied, *"Our life for yours even to death! If you do not tell this business of ours, then when the LORD gives us the land we will deal kindly and faithfully with you."*

That's *grace*! "Hang in there" until the end, and you will be saved and accepted—no matter what your parentage or nationality.

Joshua 2:15–20 and **6:22–25.** Rahab helped the spies escape that night by a rope she hung out of her window and down the city wall. As per their agreement, once she had pulled the rope back inside, Rahab immediately tied a scarlet cord in its place to mark her location.

On the day the walls of Jericho fell, Joshua sent those two spies into the rubble ahead of the rest of the troops so they could guide Rahab and her family to safety.

It's highly possible that one of those young men was a son of the leader of the tribe of Judah, for that's who married Rahab. As proof that God forgave her and accepted her as part of His people, Rahab, along with Tamar—another woman who had on one occasion been a prostitute—became great-great-grandmothers of King David and thus, of Jesus. Tamar and Rahab are two of only four women mentioned by Matthew in his listing of Jesus' genealogy. Not Eve, Sarah, Rebekah, or Leah, but former prostitutes Tamar and Rahab. God *is* in the business of forgiving.

INTO THE PROMISED LAND

Joshua 5:2–9. The spies had returned to camp on the east side of the Jordan River. At this point, we would have expected Joshua to have had the troops all primed to start conquering and settling the land, but God said they weren't ready yet. He allowed them to cross that river, at flood stage, on dry land. Then He stopped them right there, on the west side of the Jordan.

During the forty years they had been in the desert, traveling around but also marking time until the Lord's injunction was fulfilled, they had neglected to circumcise their boy babies. Therefore, just as was the case for Moses and, in a way, even for Abraham, they were not allowed to proceed until they completed that task for two or three generations of men and boys.

After they completed the circumcisions, they marched around Jericho until the walls fell.

In addition to Jericho, they conquered large sections of territory but never all of the land promised to Abraham. Then Joshua and the tribal leaders divided the country among the tribes, assigning the completion of the conquest to each individual clan.

JOSHUA'S ADMONITIONS

When Joshua was ready to retire, at the age of one hundred, he reminded them of the instructions the Lord had given concerning all the earlier inhabitants of the land of Canaan. Those commands included both the people groups already removed from the scene and the cities and villages that still remained.

Joshua 23:5–13. *"The LORD your God will push them back before you and drive them out of your sight . . . Therefore, be very strong to keep and to do all that is written in the Book of the Law of Moses . . . that you may not mix with these nations remaining among you or make mention of the names of their gods or swear by them or serve them or bow down to them, but you shall cling to the LORD your God just as you have done to this day . . . For if you turn back and cling to the remnant of these nations remaining among* *you and make marriages with them, so that you associate with them and they with you, know for certain that the LORD your God will no longer drive out these nations before you, but they shall be a snare and a trap for you, a whip on your sides and thorns in your eyes, until you perish from off this good ground that the LORD your God has given you."*

AFTER JOSHUA

The people lost interest in doing battle and decided the natives weren't perhaps quite as bad as God had told them. Therefore, they didn't get rid of all the pagan inhabitants. Those natives also kept their pornographic idols and probably their worship practices that included cult prostitution, becoming a constant temptation that the Israelites were unable to resist. And so, the Israelites took their attention away from God and relaxed their obedience to His standards. Therefore, the results were almost predictable.

Judges 3:4–6. The remaining natives *were for the testing of Israel, to know whether Israel would obey the commandments of the LORD, which he commanded their fathers by the hand of Moses. So the people of Israel lived among the Canaanites, the Hittites, the Amorites, the Perizzites, the Hivites, and the Jebusites. And their daughters they took to themselves for wives, and their own daughters they gave to their sons, and they served their gods.*

Joshua died. The entire generation, who were children when they crossed the Red Sea, died as well. The tribes, which still were not in full control of the land, became fragmented. At varying speeds, they began to neglect worship of God and took up the pornographic idols as well as the male and female prostitution practices of the native tribes they had failed to conquer. When they did, God removed His hand of blessing and allowed those tribes to be invaded by often barbaric surrounding neighbors.

After a time spent under the heel of the intruders, the Israelites finally realized the source of their problems, repented of their idolatry, and cried out to the Lord for help. Then God raised up a local leader who would become a military commander to drive out the aggressors. That leader would continue for several years in the position of judge, and the land (at least that portion of it) *had rest*[16] until the cycle started all over again.

The book of Judges is filled with snippets of this fractured history. Many of the accounts are extremely brief. Except for the pornographic nature of the Baals and Ashtaroth, only a few of those instances deal with our topic of God's message concerning sex.

CONCUBINES

We have encountered the term "concubine" before, but it bears further definition here. *Encyclopedia Britannica* says concubinage is "the state of cohabitation of a man and a woman without the full sanctions of legal marriage . . . The partners in such relationships and the offspring of their union did not have the same legal rights accorded married persons and their legitimate children."[17]

Easton's Bible Dictionary says a concubine is "a female conjugally united to a man, but in a relation inferior to that of a wife . . . a wife of secondary rank . . . They had no authority in the family, nor could they share in the household government."[18]

Thus, the woman could not have been married to someone else, for then **Leviticus 20:10** would apply and they should both have been killed.

If the man was married to someone else, the new woman became a concubine. He was still responsible for the living expenses of his wife, and, in fact, had to continue marital relations with her. He now also was liable for the living expenses of the concubine. Upon his death, the wife and/or her children would inherit his estate. The concubine got nothing.

If neither were married, the woman might still be a concubine for whom the man became financially responsible until one or the other died.

Concubinage probably most closely resembles common law marriage in our time. If so, then the commitments and responsibilities should also apply.

GIDEON

Judges 6–9. *Gideon had seventy sons, his own offspring, for he had many wives. And his concubine who was in Shechem also bore him a son.* After Gideon died, Abimelech, the son of the concubine, managed to kill all but one of those seventy other sons and started a civil war involving two major communities, declaring himself as king.

JEPHTHAH

Judges 11 tells us of Jephthah the Gileadite, who was a soldier and *the son of a prostitute.* As with the sons of Gideon, the other sons of Gilead drove Jephthah out of the territory. In this case, however, Jephthah remained faithful to the Lord and, vowing to give God whatever came out of the door of his house when he returned from a successful battle, he proceeded to lead the local tribes against the Ammonites.

He arrived home to be met by his daughter, who was his only child. While any appropriate animal (sheep, goat, or calf) would have become a burnt offering, there needed to be some other way Jephthah could fulfill his vow and still follow the rest of God's mandates. At her suggestion, the daughter was given a two-month vacation to *"go up and down on the mountains and weep for my virginity, I and my companions"* (**verse 37**). She remained a virgin for the rest of her life.

SAMSON

Judges 13–16 is the story of Samson. His parents had no children until the angel of the Lord appeared to his mother and announced that she would finally have a son, but that he was to be raised as a Nazirite, observing strict dietary laws but most especially, never, ever, having his hair cut.

After Samson grew up, he decided he wanted to marry *one of the daughters of the Philistines.* He prevailed upon his parents to make the necessary arrangements, so the wedding was planned and a feast was prepared, following the custom of the Philistines at the time. Apparently, the bride's people supplied all the rest of the wedding party. Those "companions" talked the bride into ferreting out from her new husband the secret to a parlor game riddle Samson had proposed. That left Samson owing those Philistines *"thirty linen garments and thirty changes of clothes,"* so to cover his debt, Samson went to the next town and killed thirty other Philistines, using their clothing to pay off his "companions." Then *in hot anger he went back to his father's house.* And Samson's new wife was given instead to the best man, which resulted in a major war between Samson and that group of Philistines. As part of their retaliation, the Philistines killed her and her family.

Next, Samson visited another Philistine city where he took up with a prostitute. The Philistines made several unsuccessful attempts to capture him, but each time, Samson's God-given strength allowed him to break free and walk off with everything they used against him. Then he turned instead to a third woman, Delilah. The Philistines bribed Delilah to find out how they could do away with this man who was tearing their city to pieces. She pestered Samson until he finally told her he had never had a haircut.

Delilah told her friends, and they cut Samson's hair. Then they easily overpowered him, gouged out both of his eyes, chained him, and put him in prison on a work detail. But while Samson was in prison, his hair started to grow back. More importantly, Samson stopped thinking he had done all those mighty acts under his own steam. His faith in God was renewed and therefore, his strength began to return.

The Philistines, meanwhile, gathered in a large auditorium to praise their local idol for delivering this menace into their control. They decided to add an appearance of their victim to their celebration, but Samson used that opportunity to literally pull the roof down on his captors, killing everyone in the building. Thus, God, who was in control as always, brought good out of a very mixed up situation.

THE TRIBE OF BENJAMIN

The final episode in the book of Judges is totally gory—and totally related to our theme.

Judges 19. A Levite, one allowed to help with the tabernacle activities, although not as a priest, lived in the northern part of the country. He *took to himself a concubine from Bethlehem in Judah,* which was in the middle of the nation. She left him and went back home to her father. When she had been gone several months, *her husband arose and went after her, to speak kindly to her and bring her back.* He took along one *servant and a couple of donkeys.*

The girl agreed to return to the Levite's home, but her father prevailed upon them to wait to leave until the fifth afternoon before they finally pulled out of Bethlehem. The servant wanted to spend the night in Jerusalem, which at that time, had not been taken from the native Jebusites. The Levite was reluctant to stay among foreigners, however, so they proceeded on to Gibeah, which belonged to the tribe of Benjamin.

Judges 19:16–21. The only one who offered them any hospitality was an elderly man who had been born in the northern areas but was currently living in Gibeah. *So he brought him into his house and gave the donkeys feed. And they washed their feet, and ate and drank.*

Even as they dined, a mob was forming outside.

Judges 19:22. *The men of the city, worthless fellows, surrounded the house, beating on the door. They demanded, "Bring out the man who came into your house, that we may know him."*

Beck is, as before, more explicit: *"so we may have intercourse with him."* It sounds like Sodom and Gomorrah!

Judges 19:23–24. The host tried to reason with the crowd. *"No, my brothers, do not act so wickedly; since this man has come into my house, do not do this vile thing. Behold, here are my virgin daughter and his concubine. Let me bring them out now. Violate them and do with them what seems good to you, but against this man do not do this outrageous thing."*

That suggestion had worked for Lot, but Lot and his family had benefited from the specific protection of the two guardian angels who had just visited Abraham, Lot's uncle. That most definitely didn't apply here.

Judges 19:25–26. *But the men would not listen to him. So the man seized his concubine and made her go out to them. And they knew her and abused her all night until the morning. And as the dawn began to break, they let her go. And as morning appeared, the woman came and fell down at the door of the man's house where her master was, until it was light.*

Apparently, the woman was gang-raped and otherwise abused for hours, until finally, the men of Gibeah let her escape back to the house in which she should have been staying. It seems, unlike Sodom, these individuals were willing to have intercourse with either men or women.

Judges 19:27–28. The next morning, her master prepared to resume their journey, but *when he opened the doors of the house . . . there was his concubine lying at the door of the house, with her hands on the threshold. He said to her, "Get up, let us be going." But there was no answer. Then he put her on the donkey, and the man rose up and went away to his home.*

It's unclear whether she was dead when he found her that morning or whether she died on the way home. In either case, we should be horrified by the Levite's insensitivity. And it just gets worse.

Judges 19:29. *And when he entered his house, he took a knife, and* *taking hold of his concubine he divided her, limb by limb, into twelve pieces, and sent her throughout all the territory of Israel.*

Admittedly, he wouldn't have been able to call the local TV station to come broadcast this story to the far corners of the country. He couldn't take pictures on his cell phone to post on social media. The only way he could get the word out was to actually send bits and pieces of evidence to the other tribes, along with a request for their response. So that's what he did.

Judges 19:30. *And all who saw it said, "Such a thing has never happened or been seen from the day that the people of Israel came up out of the land of Egypt until this day; consider it, take counsel, and speak."*

This, for members of the other tribes as well, was the last straw.

Judges 20:1–11. The whole nation, north to south, was up in arms. While the tribe of Benjamin sided with the inhabitants of Gibeah, 400,000 infantry soldiers from the other eleven tribes assembled at Mizpah to purge this evil from their midst.

Judges 20:12–13. *And the tribes of Israel sent men through all the tribe of Benjamin, saying, "What evil is this that has taken place among you? Now therefore give up the men, the worthless fellows in Gibeah, that we may put them to death and purge evil from Israel." But the Benjaminites would not listen.*

The eleven tribes tried to settle the matter peacefully, offering to pass sentence on only the men of the town who had perpetrated the crime. The other Benjamites, however, weren't giving an inch—never mind that their cousins were the bad guys. In response, the entire army of Benjamites took up positions inside the walls of Gibeah.

Judges 20:14–25. There were 26,700 Benjamite soldiers pitted against 400,000 from the rest of the tribes. The odds looked so overwhelming that the Israelites *inquired of God* as to which tribe should start the war. They sent only the members of the tribe of Judah into the first battle but, to their surprise, the Benjamites either killed or seriously injured 22,000 of the larger army.

Again, the Israelites prayed—this time not asking who they should bother to send, but rather, whether or not they were really in the right battle. In spite of God's answer to proceed, the second day the Israelites lost 18,000 troops.

Judges 20:26. Finally, it seems they got serious about the situation. We're told the whole Israelite army *came to Bethel and wept. They sat there before the LORD and fasted that day until evening, and offered burnt offerings and peace offerings before the LORD.*

Judges 20:28. *And the LORD said, "Go up, for tomorrow I will give them into your hand."*

The time was right because their minds and spirits had changed from revenge to a realization that in the tribe of Benjamin, there was a really bad problem that needed to be torn out by the roots.

Judges 20:29–48. The Israelites changed their battle plans, set up an ambush around the town, and because *the LORD defeated Benjamin before Israel,* they killed 25,100 Benjamites that day, besides those who had died in the earlier days of battle, and they torched the city of Gibeah. They also set fire to the other towns of Benjamin as further punishment for having taken the side of the rapists.

Judges 21. Some months later, the Israelites realized that they had not only killed all but 600 men of the tribe of Benjamin, but they had also apparently killed their wives and children. Thus, the tribe was in danger of total annihilation unless someone did something to correct the imbalance. There was just one problem: all the Israelite soldiers had pledged, because of the nature of the original crime, not to allow their daughters to marry Benjamites.

Their solution was as bizarre as the rest of this story. Realizing that no soldiers had come to the battle from the town of Jabesh in Gilead, some of those who had been in the battle were dispatched to kill all the men, boys, and married women in Jabesh, bringing all the virgin girls back to Shiloh. Then they sent notice to the remnant of the Benjamites, who came and claimed those 400 girls to be their wives.

That still left 200 potentially unmarried men. They were advised to take up positions around the town of Shiloh during a huge festival. Then, as girls and young ladies danced around the edge of the crowd, the leaders of the other 11 tribes suggested that the Benjamites should kidnap them as brides. The officials would square it with the girls' fathers.

If you aren't shaking your head already, try tracing Benjamin's line further in **1 Chronicles 8.** It's no wonder his tribe had some dysfunctional families!

At this point in history, the descendants of Abraham, Isaac, and Jacob would seem to have been a nation in total chaos. Whatever had happened to the directives they had received from God? They completely ignored Him. Suddenly, this begins to sound terribly familiar to our time.

The whole situation is best summed up in the final words of Judges:

Judges 21:25. *In those days there was no king in Israel. Everyone did what was right in his own eyes.*

What a mess!

4

IN THE DAYS OF SAMUEL, SAUL, AND DAVID

RUTH

THE BOOK OF **Ruth** actually took place during the time of the **Judges**.[19] But since Ruth became the great-grandmother of King David, it seems a more natural fit to include her with what increasingly develops as David's story. Although **Ruth 1:16** has been used as a sermon text for innumerable weddings, it was actually spoken by Ruth to her mother-in-law after Ruth's first husband had died.

To back up a bit, Naomi and her husband and two sons had left Israel during one of the famines that occurred every time God's people insisted on ignoring Him and worshiping the pornographic idols of the societies they were supposed to have obliterated (look to **Deuteronomy 27** and **28** for the reason that might have been a cause-and-effect relationship). Anyway, the family migrated to the nearby country of Moab, where the father died, the sons married, and then the sons died without producing children.

Within those ten years, the Israelites had probably returned to worshiping God because word was out that there was now an abundance of food back home. Therefore, Naomi started the long trek back to her hometown of Bethlehem. Her two daughters-in-law, possibly still teenagers, journeyed with her. Realizing these girls needed to be married again for all sorts of practical reasons, Naomi sought to release them from her family ties.

Ruth 1:11–13. *Naomi said, "Turn back, my daughters; why will you go with me?"*

She realized, and tried to convince them, that it was useless to wait for her to have other sons, then raise them to be their husbands. "Go home, girls," she was saying, "and marry one of your own people."

One girl turned and headed back to her parents. Ruth, having found in Naomi's family not only friendship and love but also a God she could trust, refused the offered retreat. That's where we get those famous words:

Ruth 1:16. *"Do not urge me to leave you or to return from following you. For where you go I will go, and where you lodge I will lodge. Your people shall be my people, and your God my God."*

So Naomi and Ruth traveled on to Bethlehem. It seems that Naomi's house was still standing, although no doubt in need of repair. They had shelter, but they needed food.

Ruth volunteered to participate in a practice that was mandated in **Leviticus 19:9–10**, designed both to feed the poor and to give them the dignity of working for that food. Israelite farmers were not to harvest the corners of their fields, but rather to leave those areas for widows, orphans, and other potentially homeless individuals. In addition, if in the remainder of the field some grain was accidentally dropped, it also was to be left for the gleaners.

The Lord led Ruth to the farms of Boaz—a cousin of her late husband. Boaz not only noticed Ruth's appearance, but he was also impressed by her devotion to Naomi. He gave his servants instructions to protect Ruth and to drop some grain on purpose where she could pick it up. He even went so far as to make sure she ate the midday meal his cooks had provided for his paid laborers.

When Naomi noticed the attention that Boaz was showering on Ruth, she decided to push matters along with a bit of matchmaking. Boaz was related closely enough to qualify for the property redemption dictates of Mosaic Law, which could also be extended to include the injunction to marry his brother's widow (**Deuteronomy 25**).

The end of any harvest season is a cause for celebration. It would seem that once they completed the ingathering of the barley crop for the year, the entire community had a festival. It must also have been customary for the owners to spend that night sleeping on the ground where they had processed the grain—whether to keep out thieves and wandering animals or merely symbolically, as a final statement that the job was done.

Ruth 3:3–4. Thus, Naomi coached Ruth to bathe, put on lotion and perfume, *"and put on your cloak and go down to the threshing floor, but do not make yourself known to the man until he has finished eating and drinking. But when he lies down, observe the place where he lies. Then go and uncover his feet and lie down, and he will tell you what to do."*

Ruth followed instructions, probably wondering what would actually happen, yet trusting that her mother-in-law knew what she was asking her to do and that the God she had come to believe in did indeed have everything under control.

Ruth 3:7–9. After feasting, which led to Boaz's good mood, he *went to lie down at the end of the heap of grain. Then she came softly and uncovered his feet and lay down. At midnight the man was startled and turned over, and behold, a woman lay at his feet! He said, "Who are you?" And she answered, "I am Ruth, your servant. Spread your wings over your servant, for you are a redeemer."* Thus, Ruth proposed to Boaz.

Boaz, who had already shown signs of being interested in just such an arrangement, had apparently been reluctant to pursue that notion, partly because he thought he was too old and therefore, thought she would probably be interested in younger men. In addition, while Boaz did indeed qualify as kinsman redeemer under Mosaic Law, a cousin could be in line ahead of him. Thus, eager though he might be, Boaz cautioned that all must be done in an orderly fashion.

Ruth 3:14. *So she lay at his feet until the morning, but arose before one* *could recognize another. And he said, "Let it not be known that the woman came to the threshing floor."*

Boaz stood guard over Ruth for the remainder of the night. Then, to preserve her reputation, he sent her home before daylight, loading her down with a generous supply of grain to take to Naomi.

Boaz immediately set out to clear the way to marry Ruth. He went straight to the city gate—the local equivalent of county court or small-town coffee shop—making sure to include in that meeting the one cousin who could take precedence to his claims.

He learned that the cousin was willing to purchase the land from Naomi, but he wasn't at all interested in marrying Ruth. That was just what Boaz wanted to hear. He would take both.

Ruth 4:9–10. *Then Boaz said to the elders and all the people, "You are witnesses this day that I have bought from the hand of Naomi all that belonged to Elimelech . . . Chilion and . . . Mahlon. Also Ruth the Moabite, the widow of Mahlon, I have bought to be my wife, to perpetuate the name of the dead in his inheritance . . ."*

Boaz received the blessing of the leaders of the community.

Ruth 4:13. *So Boaz took Ruth, and she became his wife. And he went in to her, and the LORD gave her conception, and she bore a son.*

That son, whom they named Obed, was the grandfather of King David.

And that's how Ruth, a native of the land of Moab and therefore, not an Israelite, became an ancestress of Jesus. She, along with Tamar (Judah's daughter-in-law who played the prostitute to become Judah's wife), Rahab (the prostitute who protected the spies in Jericho), Bathsheba, and Mary are the only women Matthew mentions in his listing of Jesus' pedigree. That's quite an honor!

SAMUEL

1 Samuel 1:1–11. The story of Samuel also begins with a woman. Hannah was one of two (simultaneous) wives of Elkanah, a member of the tribe of Ephraim. The other wife had borne children for Elkanah, but Hannah was barren. Not surprisingly, the other wife *used to provoke her grievously to irritate her.*

Elkanah, a pious Israelite, annually took his entire family to Shiloh for one of the three major festivals to worship and sacrifice at the tabernacle. One year, total depression overtook Hannah. Her infertility was just more than she could endure. She could neither eat nor participate in the other festivities. Crying as she approached the tabernacle, she poured out her heart to the Lord, vowing that if God would give her a son, she would *"give him to the LORD all the days of his life, and no razor shall touch his head."* In other words, the son would be a Nazirite, dedicated to God's service.

1 Samuel 1:12–16. Eli, the chief priest at the time, suspected Hannah was drunk. After she had been praying silently for a long time, Eli decided it was time to evict her. When he confronted her, however, Hannah insisted that she was instead intensely praying. She, apparently, did not reveal the content of her prayers.

1 Samuel 1:17. *Then Eli answered, "Go in peace, and the God of Israel grant your petition that you have made to him."*

1 Samuel 1:18–20. Rejoicing in that promise, no matter how off-handedly it may have been given, Hannah returned to join the rest of her family in their celebration. The next morning, they worshiped one more time at the tabernacle and headed for home where activity returned to normal—with one major change. *The LORD remembered* Hannah, and she became pregnant. She named the child Samuel, which means "God has heard."

1 Samuel 1:21–28. Instead of joining the family on their next trip to Shiloh, Hannah stayed home with Samuel until he was weaned. As with Moses, these mothers probably delayed that occasion as long as possible. Whatever Samuel's age, we are told he was *young* when Hannah brought him back to Shiloh and transferred custody of him to Eli. She revealed Samuel as the answer to her prayers and gave the little boy back to God for the rest of his life.

1 Samuel 2:19–21. Every year, Hannah made a special robe for this son she had given to the Lord, presenting it to him when the family came to the festival sacrifice. And God gave her three more sons and two daughters.

1 Samuel 3:2 and **4:18.** From the time that Hannah left him at Shiloh, Samuel was raised by High Priest Eli. While Samuel was still a boy, Eli lost his sight. Possibly some ten to fifteen years later, when Eli died, we are told that he was *old and heavy* and that *he had judged Israel forty years.*

1 Samuel 2:12–17. By the time Samuel was added to Eli's family, Eli's sons had already taken over all the priestly duties of the tabernacle. We learn *the sons of Eli were worthless men. They did not know the Lord.* One of their offenses was that they stole meat from the worshipers. The priests were allowed a portion of those parts of the animal that were sacrificed, but Eli's sons insisted on the best cuts, and fresh meat rather than cooked, instructing their servants to take all they desired—by force if necessary. I almost wonder if they were selling some of it on the side. In any case, *the sin of the young men was very great in the sight of the Lord, for the men treated the offering of the Lord with contempt.*

1 Samuel 2:22–25. *Now Eli was very old, and he kept hearing all that his sons were doing to all Israel, and how they lay with the women who were serving at the entrance to the tent of meeting. And he said to them, "Why do you do such things? For I hear of your evil dealings from all these people. No, my sons; it is no good report that I hear . . . If someone sins against a man, God will mediate for him, but if someone sins against the Lord, who can intercede for him?" But they would not* *listen to the voice of their father, for it was the will of the LORD to put them to death.*

Whether the sons were trying to instigate male cult prostitution, as practiced by ancient idol worshipers, or if they seduced and raped the women—either way, the action needed to stop. Eli apparently learned about the problem by overhearing conversations among the people who came to the tabernacle, for those worshipers might have assumed that Eli couldn't hear since he obviously couldn't see. Eli did attempt to correct his sons, but they continued to ignore him.

1 Samuel 2:27–34. So God sent a prophet to Eli to remind him of the respect required of the office of the priesthood. That prophet declared the Lord's judgment on Eli's family for their attitudes toward their positions. Not only would there be no more priests coming from Eli's line, but his two sons would soon both die in a single day.

1 Samuel 3:10–14. God gave the same message to Samuel, appearing to the boy in the middle of the night. At first, Samuel thought Eli had summoned him, but when God's call came again—and yet a third time—Eli realized God actually planned to talk directly to this young boy whose arrival at God's house had been so unusual. Once Eli convinced Samuel that it was God speaking directly to him, God told Samuel that He would *"fulfill against Eli all that I have spoken concerning his house, from beginning to end . . . I am about to punish his house forever, for the iniquity that he knew, because his sons were blaspheming God, and he did not restrain them. Therefore I swear to the house of Eli that the iniquity of Eli's house shall not be atoned for by sacrifice or offering forever."*

1 Samuel 3:15–18. The next morning, reluctantly, Samuel repeated God's message to Eli. The old man must have lived the remainder of his own life in great sorrow, realizing that not only his sons' actions but also their futures were far beyond his possibility to impact.

1 Samuel 3:19–21. *And Samuel grew, and the LORD was with him and let none of his words fall to the ground. And all Israel from*

Dan to Beersheba knew that Samuel was established as a prophet of the Lord. *And the* Lord *appeared again at Shiloh, for the* Lord *revealed himself to Samuel at Shiloh by the word of the* Lord.

We are not told how long this interval was or how old Samuel was when those prophecies were fulfilled. Since it became obvious that the Lord was speaking directly to Samuel, we might well wonder why Eli's sons didn't see the contrast and repent of their attitudes and actions, but it seems they kept to their established sinful habits.

1 Samuel 4. A major battle developed between the Israelites and the Philistines, their perpetual enemies. Apparently believing their successes in prior skirmishes had been due to the ark of the covenant rather than to the Lord Himself, the Israelites insisted that that gold-covered box should accompany them to the battlefield. This time, not only were 30,000 Israeli soldiers killed or seriously wounded but both of Eli's sons died in battle and the Philistines captured the ark. When Eli heard the news, he fell off his chair, broke his neck, and died the same day.

1 Samuel 7. Finally, twenty years after the ark had been temporarily kidnapped and then returned, God's people began to turn their attention once more to Him. Samuel declared a time of total cleanup and repentance:

1 Samuel 7:3–4. *And Samuel said to all the house of Israel, "If you are returning to the* Lord *with all your heart, then put away the foreign gods and the Ashtaroth from among you and direct your heart to the* Lord *and serve him only, and he will deliver you out of the hand of the Philistines." So the people of Israel put away the Baals and the Ashtaroth, and they served the* Lord *only.*

Whether the Israelites pulverized those pornographic idols or merely buried them in the trash, many of the peoples who had originated those false deities were still in the land. Those Philistines and other clans continued in their native practices, always influencing God's people away from worship of the Lord. Thus, those same idolatrous names show up time and again from this point until the Babylonian exile.

1 Samuel 8. *When Samuel became old, he made his sons judges over Israel . . . Yet his sons did not walk in his ways but turned aside after gain. They took bribes and perverted justice.*

Therefore, the citizenry started clamoring to have a king, *"like all the nations."* Samuel took that as a personal affront, but God explained it was really the Lord Himself they were rejecting, not Samuel. It was time to establish a more permanent governmental structure than they had in place under the judges, one that would include standing armies—and taxes—and rules made and enforced by the whim of the one who was in charge.

KING SAUL

1 Samuel 9 and **10.** Think back to the tribe of Benjamin, which nearly got wiped out in the closing pages of **Judges.** Their account was the last one reviewed in our prior chapter. It's interesting that Benjamin was the tribe from which their first king was to come. We are told Saul was *a handsome young man. There was not a man among the people of Israel more handsome than he. From his shoulders upward he was taller than any of the people.* If they wanted a movie star, Saul would be the one. In addition, his family was wealthy. He fit exactly what they were asking for.

The record of Saul's reign contains very few items relevant to our study of *God's Word about Sex.* Saul, apparently, had only one wife, who I'm guessing didn't deserve the description hurled at Jonathan in **1 Samuel 20:30.** We really shouldn't be surprised that King Saul's words sound a lot like we hear from people with a foul mouth in America today.

Saul also had a concubine, but we don't read about her until after Saul's death.

Most of what we're given in the remainder of **1 Samuel** is actually related to David, who was anointed to be king many years before Saul ceased to be the reigning monarch.

KING SAUL AND DAVID

1 Samuel 17. You're probably familiar with the account of David and Goliath, that "*uncircumcised Philistine*" who had defied "*the armies of the living God.*" Even there, sex played a role.

King Saul, who was a full head taller than his subjects, should have been a match to fight Goliath. Instead, Saul offered his daughter in marriage to whoever would kill the giant, with an exemption from taxes thrown in besides.

1 Samuel 18. Eventually, Saul got around to an attempt at keeping his rash promise. He first announced that his oldest daughter could be David's wife, but when David didn't immediately take the king up on the deal, Saul gave the girl to someone else.

Saul's daughter, Michal, had meanwhile developed a crush on this young warrior. King Saul, already insanely jealous of David's popularity arising from his military victories, hoped that a bride would slow the younger man down enough so the Philistines would kill him. Saul put out the word that Michal could marry David.

In an era when grooms had to pay a bride price to their prospective fathers-in-law, David, as the youngest of eight sons, had neither ready cash nor hopes of a healthy inheritance. But Saul didn't want money. He wanted David killed, the sooner the better, especially if that death would seem a natural outcome of fighting.

1 Samuel 18:25–27. So Saul told his servants to tell David, "*The king desires no bride-price except a hundred foreskins of the Philistines, that he may be avenged of the king's enemies.*" *Now Saul thought to make David fall by the hand of the Philistines . . . Before the time had expired, David arose* *and went, along with his men, and killed two hundred of the Philistines. And David brought their foreskins, which were given in full number to the king, that he might become the king's son-in-law. And Saul gave him his daughter Michal for a wife.*

Gross! Gruesome, even! I don't suppose there was any other way to prove headcount, and that particular chunk of skin would certainly attest to the nationality of those he'd killed, but really!

1 Samuel 19 and **25:44.** As God allowed *a harmful spirit* to enter the king's life, Saul grew more and more jealous, and finally attempted to have David arrested. Warned and assisted by Michal, Saul's daughter but also David's wife, David escaped this ambush by leaving home on a rope through the window, just as his ancestor had left Rahab's home in the time of Joshua. In this case, however, it appears that Michal and David were separated for several years while David roamed the countryside, always one step ahead of Saul. Perhaps as a sort of retaliation, Saul arranged for Michal to marry somebody else.

1 Samuel 21. When David escaped from Saul's henchmen, he first traveled to the tabernacle, hoping, perhaps, to get some assistance from Samuel, but Samuel wasn't there at the time. One of the statements David made on that occasion is actually pertinent to our study. Giving the priest on duty an excuse to allow David to appropriate the showbread that was supposed to only be eaten by priests, he explains:

1 Samuel 21:5. *"Truly women have been kept from us as always when I go on an expedition."*

Unlike armies of that and later times, David did not take along camp followers as part of his troops. History records camp followers of some armies that included cooks, launderers, and nurses—but also prostitutes.[20]

1 Samuel 25. Once it became clear that Saul would continue to chase David for years, apparently David expanded his clandestine encampments to include soldiers' families—possibly because those families would also be subject to harassment from government forces. And David began to take other wives.

David and his ever-increasing entourage were constantly on the run, never sure whether the allegiances of any town would stay with David or revert to Saul, the reigning monarch. They lived off the land and were assisted by the locals whenever they were in friendly territory. In exchange, the troops helped the local shepherds patrol their pastures, getting rid of predators and standing watch over the flocks while they guarded their own encampments.

One of the rich landowners whose immense flocks had been so protected was Nabal, whose name, we are told, meant "stupid." We are also told *the man was harsh and badly behaved,* which seems to indicate he was abusive. A listing of his family tree, in **1 Chronicles 2:18–29** and **46–50**, explains part of Nabal's background. His wife, Abigail, was *discerning and beautiful.*

At sheep-shearing time, David sent ten soldiers to the festivities, which always followed such occasions, requesting provisions for his army. Nabal refused their request, which brought the threat of retaliation from the troops. A servant reported the situation to Abigail, who assembled an abundance of food. Then she and her household servants secretly delivered the supplies to David. That averted what could have been a very messy battle between Israelite factions.

The next day, when Abigail informed Nabal of her actions, he had a heart attack from which he died ten days later. *Then David sent and spoke to Abigail, to take her as his wife.*

David also had another wife in camp at the time, Ahinoam of Jezreel. We aren't told how long they remained vagabonds, even living in Philistine territory for a time. David had been anointed king while he was a mere youth, but he didn't get to actually be king until after some political maneuverings following the death of King Saul.

2 Samuel 3. Here we learn about Rizpah, Saul's concubine. After Saul and most of his sons died in battle, Abner, the commander of Saul's army, had intercourse with Rizpah. That led to a major feud between Abner and Saul's remaining son Ish-bosheth, resulting in a shift of Abner's allegiance from Ish-bosheth to David. No longer protected by Abner, Ish-bosheth became an easy target for two men who slipped into his bedroom and killed him while he slept.[21]

DAVID AS KING

2 Samuel 3:2–5, 14–16. Apparently, David fathered no children as long as Saul was alive. During the seven years he reigned from Hebron, David took on four more wives. While at Hebron, each of his six wives gave birth to a son. David also sent messengers to Saul's heirs, demanding that his first wife Michal be returned to him. Michal's new husband was most reluctant to give her up but did so at Abner's insistence.

2 Samuel 5. After seven and a half years in Hebron, David captured Jerusalem and declared it his capital. We are told he *took more concubines and wives from Jerusalem* and had several more children. **1 Chronicles 3:1–9** and **14:3–7** list six sons born in Hebron, then four sons by Bathsheba, nine other sons in Jerusalem, one daughter, and (mentioned but not counted) other sons by his concubines. It was definitely a full palace!

2 Samuel 6. After David had established his reign in Jerusalem, completely taking over the city, he decided that the political capital of his kingdom should also be its religious capital. He, therefore, determined to have the ark of the covenant moved to Jerusalem, even though the tabernacle would still remain in Shiloh.

As part of the festive ceremony in which the ark finally arrived, *David danced before the* LORD *with all his might . . .* [He] *was wearing a linen ephod,* which was a sort of shoulder to hip garment worn by the priests, usually over several other layers of clothing. It is possible that David was fully covered, in spite of Michal's statement in **2 Samuel 6:20:** *Michal the daughter of Saul came out to meet David and said, "How the king of Israel honored himself today, uncovering himself today before the eyes of his servants' female servants, as one of the vulgar fellows shamelessly uncovers himself!"*

Fill in more of the blanks with Ezra's recounting of the same event:

1 Chronicles 15:27. *David was clothed with a robe of fine linen, as also were all the Levites who were carrying the ark, and the singers and Chenaniah the leader of the music of the singers. And David wore a linen ephod.*

It's possible that David temporarily abandoned that part of his outfit as he led the procession uphill for those several miles or that perhaps the robe he wore wasn't one of the more royal garments. In either case, David was decently covered.

2 Samuel 6:23. *And Michal the daughter of Saul had no child to the day of her death.*

Men don't take lightly to a loss of respect. In return for her possibly jealous remarks, it would seem that David crossed her off his list of candidates for intercourse, even though she was apparently not allowed to return to the man to whom King Saul had given her after she helped David escape from Saul's soldiers.

None of Saul's descendants were able to establish themselves as king. God promised David, however, that not only would one of his sons follow him on the throne, but that down the line, someone inheriting David's DNA would rule forever.

2 Samuel 7:12–16. God promised that, when David's earthly life ended, "*I will raise up your offspring after you, who shall come from your body, and I will establish his kingdom . . . I will be to him a father, and he shall be to me a son . . . And your house and your kingdom shall be made sure forever before me. Your throne shall be established forever.*'"

The only way that promise could be fulfilled would be with a human (coming from David's DNA) who would also be God (in order to be eternal). We're even told of the Father/Son relationship articulated by Jesus in the New Testament. It's interesting to note that David was the last person in the Old Testament to whom that messianic promise was given.

Sometime after David had established his rule in Jerusalem, a neighboring king died. Apparently, that Ammonite king had been friendly to David in the days when he was constantly fleeing from King Saul, for David sent ambassadors to his son with a message of condolence. But that son's cabinet members accused David's men of being spies.

2 Samuel 10:4. As punishment, *Hanun took David's servants and shaved off half the beard of each and cut off their garments in the middle, at their hips, and sent them away.*

Mini-miniskirts and half-and-half beards! That's no way to treat an ambassador! No doubt, Hanun's soldiers also provided a very public escort all the way to the border.

David's envoys were mortified. While proper covering would have been provided immediately once the men crossed back into Israel, they were too embarrassed to even attempt a return to Jerusalem until their beards grew out. The war was on.

2 Samuel 10:6–19. So the Ammonites hired the Syrians and a few of the smaller tribes north and east of Israel. David and his commanding general, Joab, each led an army against the amassed other nations, killing thousands. The end result was that those foreign rulers *made peace with Israel and became subject to them.*

2 Samuel 11:1a. *In the spring of the year, the time when kings go out to battle, David sent Joab, and his servants with him, and all Israel. And they ravaged the Ammonites and besieged Rabbah.*[22]

The next spring should have been fairly peaceful, at least to the north and east of the kingdom. King David needed to send a reminder to the Ammonites so they didn't start another war, but his heart wasn't really in that campaign. After all, trouncing a nation once should be enough.

The Israelites were on the offense, not defense. Nevertheless, the phrase *the time when kings go out to battle,* although, no doubt, totally accurate, makes me think spring military campaigns might have been as much a testosterone declaration as anything else. Weather, of course, would have also played a part.

2 Samuel 11:1b. *But David remained at Jerusalem . . .*

Normal procedure would have been for a king to lead his troops into battle. David had been fighting wars and skirmishes ever since he killed

Goliath, but this time, he chose to stay home and just send out his army to punish the Ammonites.

The king was bored. He, no doubt, wished he had gone out to lead the troops—or even that he could go out to the hills with a flock of sheep. A game of touch football with his palace guards would have been helpful, but that hadn't been invented yet.

DAVID, URIAH, AND BATHSHEBA

2 Samuel 11:2a. *It happened, late one afternoon, when David arose from his couch and was walking on the roof of the king's house . . .*

A king couldn't just go out and prowl the streets. Even in fairly peaceful times, that would have required a Secret Service detail—and a reason for going wherever. The palace roof was flat, giving him some space to pace, but David would have been frustrated after a few rounds. People didn't just exercise for the sake of exercising. Not in those days, when nearly everyone had to walk everywhere they went. A movement caught his eye:

2 Samuel 2b. *He saw from the roof a woman bathing; and the woman was very beautiful.*

Castles and palaces are normally built on the highest ground around, not only for defense but also for the psychological advantage that the king had as he looked down on his subjects. In a nation with flat roofs, people actually considered that area to be living space because it was the coolest part of the house. It would seem that Bathsheba's bathing spot was not completely shielded from those whose location was above her. Thus, her naked body could easily be seen from the palace.

2 Samuel 11:3. *And David sent and inquired about the woman. And one said, "Is not this Bathsheba, the daughter of Eliam, the wife of Uriah the Hittite?"*

David already had several wives. The information that Bathsheba was already married should have stopped all further thought on the subject. In fact, David knew her husband—one of the group of thirty special forces of David's army—quite possibly a loyal soldier who had been with David's troops for many years.

2 Samuel 11:4. *So David sent messengers and took her, and she came to him, and he lay with her. (Now she had been purifying herself from her uncleanness.) Then she returned to her house.*

Bathsheba had just completed her seven-day menstrual period isolation, as per **Leviticus 15.** Had Uriah's household been poorer, she would have had to use the communal bath down the street, out of range of David's vision. In any case, although he now knew she was married to someone else, David sent servants to her house to summon Bathsheba—not to court but to the royal bedchamber. We're not told whether or not she protested. In any case, a king was a ruler so you didn't argue with him. Intercourse occurred. Then, when he was finished, David sent her back home.

2 Samuel 11:5. *And the woman conceived, and she sent and told David, "I am pregnant."*

Bathsheba probably waited until after her second missed cycle to send the message to the palace. After all, for something this important, it paid to be certain. That she had become pregnant is not surprising, given the timing of their encounter. In any case, now some of Bathsheba's servants—and some of David's servants—knew with certainty what had occurred behind those closed doors.

2 Samuel 11:6. *So David sent word to Joab, "Send me Uriah the Hittite." And Joab sent Uriah to David.*

Never mind that the exposure should never have happened or that the baby was actually a child of the king. David merely wanted to cover his tracks. It does remind me of the unfortunate modern theory that intercourse without commitment is fine—it's just any resulting pregnancy that our culture defines as wrong.

2 Samuel 11:7. *When Uriah came to him, David asked how Joab was doing and how the people were doing and how the war was going.*

A cover story had to be developed so everyone would think Uriah was just a randomly selected messenger sent to keep the king informed.

2 Samuel 11:8. *Then David said to Uriah, "Go down to your house and wash your feet." And Uriah went out of the king's house, and there followed him a present from the king.*

I can almost hear David thinking, "Gee, thanks for coming! Go home and relax, and I'll let you know when I have a return message for you to take back." David even included a bonus for Uriah, or so it would have appeared to the public. In fact, it was likely the payment of a guilty conscience.

2 Samuel 11:9. *But Uriah slept at the door of the king's house with all the servants of his lord, and did not go down to his house.*

Uriah was apparently a soldier first and a husband second. He considered himself still on duty, prepared to be sent back to the battle at any moment. He didn't go home. So David's cover was not established.

2 Samuel 11:10. *When they told David, "Uriah did not go down to his house," David said to Uriah, "Have you not come from a journey? Why did you not go down to your house?"*

Again, I almost hear David thinking, "I dismissed you! Go home and have sex with your wife!"

2 Samuel 11:11. *Uriah said to David, "The ark and Israel and Judah dwell in booths, and my lord Joab and the servants of my lord are camping in the open field. Shall I then go to my house, to eat and to drink and to lie with my wife? As you live, and as your soul lives, I will not do this thing."*

That Uriah mentions the ark first seems to indicate that, though as a Hittite he was a foreigner, Uriah may well have been a believer in the God of Abraham. In any case, his reasoning was that the entire army was out in the field, therefore, he was still on duty. We might even suspect some of the troops, including Uriah, were wondering why the commander in chief wasn't with them.

2 Samuel 11:12. *Then David said to Uriah, "Remain here today also, and tomorrow I will send you back." So Uriah remained in Jerusalem that day and the next.*

David obviously didn't have his act together. That far removed from the battlefield, he had no words of wisdom to send his general. David had painted himself into a corner.

2 Samuel 11:13. *And David invited him, and he ate in his presence and drank, so that he made him drunk. And in the evening he went out to lie on his couch with the servants of his lord, but he did not go down to his house.*

Uriah didn't take the bait, even though the king made sure his soldier got drunk. Uriah maintained his attitude of active duty.

2 Samuel 11:14–15. *In the morning David wrote a letter to Joab and sent it by the hand of Uriah. In the letter he wrote, "Set Uriah in the forefront of the hardest fighting, and then draw back from him, that he may be struck down, and die."*

Thus, David sent Uriah back to the front, carrying his own death sentence. And David added murder to adultery.

2 Samuel 11:16–17. *And as Joab was besieging the city, he assigned Uriah to the place where he knew there were valiant men. And the men of the city came out and fought with Joab, and some of the servants of David among the people fell. Uriah the Hittite also died.*

The order had been clear. Arrange for the assassination of Uriah, but make it look like a normal casualty of war. While Joab followed orders, he must have wondered why the king wanted to kill one of his better soldiers.

2 Samuel 11:18–24. Joab sent word back to King David, "Mission accomplished." In fact, Joab expressly instructed the messenger that, should there be any royal static over the way the battle was waged, the mention of the death of Uriah should calm any ruffled imperial feathers.

2 Samuel 11:25. David's message back to Joab was simply, *"Do not let this matter displease you, for the sword devours now one and now another. Strengthen your attack against the city and overthrow it."*

"Oh, OK. Sounds good. Carry on!" I can almost hear David's sigh of relief.

2 Samuel 11:26–27a. *When the wife of Uriah heard that Uriah her husband was dead, she lamented over her husband. And when the mourning* *was over, David sent and brought her to his house, and she became his wife and bore him a son.*

When Bathsheba arrived at the palace, she was probably three months pregnant. When the baby—by no means a preemie—was born six months later, every adult, either part of the court or one of the servants, would have known there was something fishy going on.

2 Samuel 11:27b. *But the thing that David had done displeased the LORD.*

This is the true bottom line here. However we may hurt or harm our neighbor, ultimately, our sin is against God.

2 Samuel 12:1. But God didn't leave it there. As He does with each of us, when we sin, He works to get our attention and draw us back to Him. In this case, the Lord sent the prophet Nathan to confront the king with a parable:

2 Samuel 12:1–4. *"There were two men in a certain city, the one rich and the other poor. The rich man had very many flocks and herds, but the poor man had nothing but one little ewe lamb, which he had bought."* The lamb had become not only a household pet, but almost a member of the family. *". . . Now there came a traveler to the rich man, and he was unwilling to take one of his own flock or herd to prepare for the guest who had come to him, but he took the poor man's lamb and prepared it for the man who had come to him."*

2 Samuel 12:5–6. David angrily retorted, *"As the LORD lives, the man who has done this deserves to die, and he shall restore the lamb fourfold, because he did this thing, and because he had no pity."*

David could easily see the total unfairness of the rich man's actions. He didn't yet see the parallels—that his abuse of eminent domain was much worse and that he broke commandments all over the place besides. The penalty David suggested was the highest allowed under Hebrew law.

2 Samuel 12:7a. *Nathan said to David, "You are the man!"*

This, then, was the application. It wasn't just a story for the sake of telling stories. This was a message straight from God, by the mouth of the prophet.

2 Samuel 12:7b–9. *"Thus says the L*ORD*, the God of Israel, 'I anointed you king over Israel, and I delivered you out of the hand of Saul. And I gave you your master's house and your master's wives into your arms and gave you the house of Israel and of Judah. And if this were too little, I would add to you as much more. Why have you despised the word of the L*ORD*, to do what is evil in his sight? You have struck down Uriah the Hittite with the sword and have taken his wife to be your wife and have killed him with the sword of the Ammonites.'"*

David may have thought he was hiding his tracks, even though several others had been involved in the plot. But God knew all the gory details.

2 Samuel 12:10–12. *"'Now therefore the sword shall never depart from your house, because you have despised me and have taken the wife of Uriah the Hittite to be your wife.' Thus says the L*ORD*, 'Behold, I will raise up evil against you out of your own house. And I will take your wives before your eyes and give them to your neighbor, and he shall lie with your wives in the sight of this sun. For you did it secretly, but I will do this thing before all Israel.'"*

Again, the ultimate infraction was against God Himself.[23] It's in our attitude toward Him that we make the decisions to do wrong, thus, our breaking of any of the commandments is really throwing aside God's rules and replacing them with our own ideas, in essence, elevating ourselves above the Creator of the universe.

As we learned from the accounts of Jacob, Abraham, and Adam, sins can be forgiven but they still bear consequences in the here and now. David's own son, Absalom, would be the one to fulfill this prophecy.

2 Samuel 12:13. *David said to Nathan, "I have sinned against the L*ORD*." And Nathan said to David, "The L*ORD *also has put away your sin; you shall not die."*

Confession. Absolution. Forgiveness.

2 Samuel 12:14. *"Nevertheless, because by this deed you have utterly scorned the L*ORD*, the child who is born to you shall die."*

This consequence would affect both David and Bathsheba, for both had known their original action was wrong, but they went ahead and did it anyway.

2 Samuel 12:15–23. The child, whose name and age are never given, soon became sick. David fasted and prayed earnestly, but at the end of seven days, in accordance with the prophecy, the child died. When that happened, knowing that God's verdict was final, David rose, bathed, and ate again.

2 Samuel 12:24. *Then David comforted his wife, Bathsheba, and went in to her and lay with her, and she bore a son, and he called his name Solomon.*

Although younger than several of David's other sons, Solomon—the son of his now-favorite wife—would be the one David picked to follow him on the throne.

AMNON AND TAMAR

God had forgiven David's coveting, adultery, and murder, but the consequences of his actions would long reverberate within David's family. As the oldest of David's sons reached young adulthood, frictions increased among the number of sub-households resulting from David's several wives and concubines.

2 Samuel 13:1. *Now Absalom, David's son, had a beautiful sister, whose name was Tamar. And after a time Amnon, David's son, loved her.*

Amnon's mother was Ahinoam from Jezreel. Probably a native Israelite, Ahinoam was the first woman David married while he was actively pursued by King Saul (**1 Samuel 25:43**). Amnon was David's firstborn son, and, therefore, should have been heir apparent. Absalom, the third son born in Hebron, was also the grandson of the king of Geshur.[24] It is doubtful that the people of Geshur believed in the God of Abraham, Isaac, and Jacob. Amnon developed a crush on Absalom's sister Tamar, which qualified as an incestuous relationship according to **Leviticus 18:9.**

Unfortunately, Hebrew, like English, expects the word "love" to cover a multitude of emotions. Thus, you love chocolate, your grandmother, your spouse, God, and beautiful sunsets. In this case, instead of the brotherly feelings he should have had, Amnon let his hormones take over.

2 Samuel 13:2. *And Amnon was so tormented that he made himself ill because of his sister Tamar, for she was a virgin, and it seemed impossible to Amnon to do anything to her.*

We almost get the impression that Tamar, as perhaps one of few girls in a family of many boys, had always been treated like the princess she truly was. Tamar was probably protected by a crowd of big brothers as well as servants and their version of the Secret Service. After all, daughters of kings were often married off to surrounding potentates as political maneuvers. All that factored in, in addition to the expectation that a bride would be a virgin until her wedding night. **Deuteronomy 22** tells us that proof could even be made public. It's no wonder Amnon couldn't find a way to be alone with her.

She was beautiful—and off-limits. That combination was enough to make Amnon's testosterone levels go through the roof.

2 Samuel 13:3–4a. Amnon's cousin Jonadab, *a very crafty man,* suggested, *"O son of the king, why are you so haggard morning after morning? Will you not tell me?"*

Jonadab had developed a friendship with this heir-apparent to the throne. I wonder if he was hoping for a position in a future administration. Or it may have been merely out of friendship that he inquired, "Hey, buddy, you're losing sleep over something. Let me help you fix it."

2 Samuel 13:4b. *Amnon said to him, "I love Tamar, my brother Absalom's sister."*

This was more than a crush. It had turned to lust.

2 Samuel 13:5. Jonadab answered, *"Lie down on your bed and pretend to be ill. And when your father comes to see you, say to him, 'Let my sister Tamar come and give me bread to eat, and prepare the food in my sight, that I may see it and eat it from her hand.'"*

Jonadab added fuel to the fire that was already raging in Amnon's hormones. "What you really need, cousin, is to get that girl into your bed. Here's an excuse you can use to get the king to send her to you. Then you take it from there."

2 Samuel 13:6–7. *So Amnon lay down and pretended to be ill. And when the king came to see him, Amnon said to the king, "Please let my sister Tamar come and make a couple of cakes in my sight, that I may eat from her hand." Then David sent home to Tamar, saying, "Go to your brother Amnon's house and prepare food for him."*

Amnon put the plot in motion. David fell for the story, not asking why Tamar's cooking was supposedly so much better than that of the royal chefs. Note that Amnon was no longer living in the royal palace, which would suggest he might have been twenty or older.

2 Samuel 13:8–9. *So Tamar went to her brother Amnon's house, where he was lying down. And she . . . made cakes in his sight and baked the cakes. And she took the pan and emptied it out before him, but he refused to eat. And Amnon said, "Send out everyone from me." So everyone went out from him.*

Quite possibly, Tamar was a bit flattered at this attention from big brother. In any case, she didn't seem to suspect anything sinister at this point. Her attitude seemed to be, "Humor him. He thinks he's sick. He probably just stubbed his toe, but these silly brothers of mine need pampering every once in a while."

2 Samuel 13:10. *Then Amnon said to Tamar, "Bring the food into the chamber, that I may eat from your hand." And Tamar took the cakes she had made and brought them into the chamber to Amnon her brother.*

She still didn't suspect his motives.

2 Samuel 13:11. *But when she brought them near him to eat, he took hold of her and said to her, "Come, lie with me, my sister."*

When Amnon grabbed Tamar, suddenly, the game was over. The teasing big brother was turning into a rapist.

2 Samuel 13:12. *She answered him, "No, my brother, do not violate me, for such a thing is not done in Israel; do not do this outrageous thing."*

Tamar's reaction was quick: "Stop! Don't rape me!" While that might have been a common practice in other nations, they both knew Israel had strong laws regarding rape. At the very least, **Exodus 22:16–17** and **Deuteronomy 22:28–29** would have applied. Beck makes her words even stronger: *"Don't do such an ungodly thing!"*

2 Samuel 13:13. Tamar continued, *"As for me, where could I carry my shame? And as for you, you would be as one of the outrageous fools in Israel. Now therefore, please speak to the king, for he will not withhold me from you."*

Her good name would be ruined, but so would Amnon's. The bad reputation would have followed him to the throne, had he lived that long. But neither remembered that this would be incest as well as rape. Tamar's comment that King David would give Amnon anything he wanted seems to totally ignore that aspect of the equation.

2 Samuel 13:14. *But he would not listen to her, and being stronger than she, he violated her and lay with her.*

Never mind Tamar's protests—or possibly even her screams for help. Amnon overpowered and raped his half sister.

2 Samuel 13:15–17. *Then Amnon hated her with very great hatred, so that the hatred . . . was greater than the love with which he had loved her. And Amnon said to her, "Get up! Go!" But she said to him, "No, my brother, for this wrong in sending me away is greater than the other that you did to me." But he would not listen to her. He called the young man who served him and said, "Put this woman out of my presence and bolt the door after her."*

Having had intercourse with Tamar, Amnon totally lost respect for her. In fact, he couldn't even stand the sight of her. "Kick her out into the street, and make sure she never comes back."

Ladies, beware. That reaction is not so unusual. "I want your body. Oh, it wasn't that great after all. Go away, I don't ever want to see you again."

2 Samuel 13:18–19. *Now she was wearing a long robe with sleeves, for thus were the virgin daughters of the king dressed. So his servant put her out and bolted the door after her. And Tamar put ashes on her head and tore the long robe that she wore. And she laid her hand on her head and went away, crying aloud as she went.*

Tamar was devastated. The ashes and tearing of her royal robe, in particular, were normal signs of mourning in that culture. Her appearance—probably quite disheveled—plus her loud cries—would have made the episode public.

ABSALOM

2 Samuel 13:20. *And her brother Absalom said to her, "Has Amnon your brother been with you? Now hold your peace, my sister. He is your brother; do not take this to heart." So Tamar lived, a desolate woman, in her brother Absalom's house.*

Absalom's reaction is not what we would have expected from a big brother. Already coveting the throne, he saw this as an excuse to depose his older brother, or perhaps to get rid of him even sooner. He totally ignored Tamar's feelings and needs. She became merely a pawn in Absalom's scheme of political intrigue.

2 Samuel 13:21. *When King David heard of all these things, he was very angry.*

King David was angry, but he didn't do anything. His own actions with Bathsheba had set a bad example for his family, and David knew he was now reaping the consequences. And this would be just the beginning of his family troubles.

2 Samuel 13:22. Absalom publicly ignored Amnon while hating him for violating Tamar. While he seemed to not be reacting to the rape, actually Absalom was plotting his revenge.

2 Samuel 13:23–27. Two years later, the dominos were all in place. Absalom invited his father and all his brothers to a sheep-shearing festivity. When the king demurred, thinking an invasion by the royal court would be too great a financial and logistical burden for his son, Absalom narrowed his guest list to simply Amnon and the other brothers.

2 Samuel 13:28. The stage was set. Absalom instructed his servants to watch while he got Amnon drunk, then kill big brother.

2 Samuel 13:29–36. While it was only Amnon whose life was in danger, the rest of the brothers immediately fled back to Jerusalem. The first rumor reaching King David was that all his sons had been killed. Jonadab, the same cousin who had encouraged Amnon into raping Tamar (but who was apparently still allowed at court), guessed correctly that this was Absalom's revenge for that event, reassuring David that not all of his sons had been murdered.

2 Samuel 13:37—14:33. Absalom fled immediately to the country of his mother's people, where he stayed for three years. By then King David had ceased to mourn for Amnon, his oldest son, and started missing Absalom. So David officially pardoned Absalom, allowing him to return to Jerusalem, but did not receive him at court for two more years.

2 Samuel 15 and **16.** Patience was never Absalom's strong suit. He coveted the throne, never mind that there was still one brother ahead of him in age. In fact, he wanted it now, not content to wait until his father died. He used his movie star appearance (**2 Samuel 14:25–26**) to gather the support of the population, including some of the religious and military leaders.

Four years after he had returned to Jerusalem, Absalom arranged to have himself declared king at Hebron, the city where David had begun his reign. Rather than fight his son, David chose to evacuate his people out of Jerusalem—except for the ten concubines he left to take care of the palace, one aged cabinet member, and the chief priest and his sons, who David sent back into the city to provide information as to what was going on, and if possible to give bad advice to Absalom and his followers.

2 Samuel 16:20. *Then Absalom said to Ahithophel, "Give your counsel. What shall we do?"* Ahithophel had been an advisor to King David. Combining **2 Samuel 23:34** with 2 **Samuel 11:3,** it's possible he was also Bathsheba's grandfather, and thus, had some rather bad feelings toward David. In any case, he sided with Absalom, becoming one of his chief consultants.

2 Samuel 16:21–22. *Ahithophel said to Absalom, "Go in to your father's concubines, whom he has left to keep the house, and all Israel will hear that you have made yourself a stench to your father, and the hands of all who are with you will be strengthened." So they pitched a tent for Absalom on the roof. And Absalom went in to his father's concubines in the sight of all Israel.*

And the sin came full circle. On the same rooftop from which King David had first noticed Bathsheba, his son Absalom now had a tent pitched where Beck says *he had intercourse with his father's concubines in the sight of Israel.* Not just one, but he publicly raped all ten concubines who had been left behind. In this case, that rape also included incest, for they qualified as being Absalom's father's wives. What a mess!

Following a hasty and difficult flight from Jerusalem to the other side of the Jordan River, the forces loyal to King David regrouped and, under the leadership of Joab, engaged in battle with the soldiers following Absalom. In the ensuing battle, Absalom's long hair got caught in a tree while his mule trotted on without him, making him an easy target. Commander Joab was the one who killed Absalom, even though King David had pleaded for mercy for his errant son.

KING DAVID'S FINAL DAYS

2 Samuel 20:3. *So David and the rest of his household returned to the palace. And the king took the ten concubines whom he had left to care for the house and put them in a house under guard and provided for them, but did not go in to them. So they were shut up until the day of their death, living as if in widowhood.*

With the battle over, when David got back home, he had the ten concubines removed from the palace, barred from court, and possibly put under house arrest for as long as they lived. Absalom's actions with them hadn't been their fault, but to have returned to normal relations with them would have compounded the problem of incest.

Sex even colored the final days of King David's life:

1 Kings 1:1–4. *Now King David was old and advanced in years. And although they covered him with clothes, he could not get warm. Therefore his servants said to him, "Let a young woman be sought for my lord the king, and let her wait on the king and be in his service. Let her lie in your arms, that my lord the king may be warm." So they sought for a beautiful young woman throughout all the territory of Israel, and found Abishag the Shunammite, and brought her to the king. The young woman was very beautiful, and she was of service to the king and attended to him, but the king knew her not.*

Abishag was King David's nurse, but she was chosen for her probable ability to stimulate David's testosterone levels rather than for her medical skills. They did not have intercourse.

So ended the physical life—and reign—of King David. Specially chosen while he was still a young boy, beloved by God, blessed beyond measure in his leadership skills and popularity, but like all of us, David had feet of clay. He was human. He made mistakes, especially in his relationship with Bathsheba. Yet God forgave them both and allowed them to be human ancestors of Jesus.

5

THE REST OF THE KINGS

THE BOOKS OF **1 and 2 Kings** pick up the history from King David's final days and King Solomon's coronation through the split of the descendants of Jacob into a Northern Kingdom, which retained the name of Israel, and a Southern Kingdom, which kept the monarchy of David's descendants but took the name of Judah (or sometimes Judea). That history ends with the deportation of Judah to Babylon. While we learn very little about some dynasties and quite a bit about others, the books of the Kings also recount the ministries of the prophets Elijah and Elisha, who both worked in the Northern Kingdom.

Following that, the books of **1 and 2 Chronicles** give us a condensed version of the history of Judah only, starting with Adam. Since a great deal in those two books is repetition of the four that precede them, we will review them in combination with the longer versions.

In many cases, the only information we have that is pertinent to our topic is that the pornographic idols of Baal and Ashtoreth were still present and still leading people away from the Lord. For other kings, we have pages of information. Thus, this study will pick out the nuggets as they relate to our topic and ignore the other eras and rulers.

Although there were other idols worshiped, the common threads running through most of the reigns of the bad kings were the Baals and Ashtoreths. Here's what was so wrong about these idols and why coexistence with them was so dangerous:

- They were pornographic.
- Their worship often involved prostitution.
- Most important of all, in place of worshiping God, they substituted the worship of sex.

No wonder the Lord got angry!

SOLOMON

Even before King David died, Solomon was crowned king of what was then a still-united country. His coronation was not without incident though. His brothers, Amnon and Absalom, had been killed, and we never hear any more about David's second son (Chileab, son of Abigail). But Solomon's fourth oldest brother, Adonijah, had declared himself king. So David took charge of the situation, fulfilled his promise to Bathsheba, and made sure her son Solomon was installed on the throne.

1 Kings 2:12–25. Prince Adonijah, however, did not go quietly into oblivion. He requested Solomon's mother to ask the king that he be allowed to marry Abishag the Shunammite, the woman who had been David's nurse and bed warmer for his final days. Even though David and Abishag didn't have intercourse, there was still the appearance of closeness. If Abishag had been given to Adonijah, it would have implied her new partner was the equivalent of the man she had been available for before—the king. Solomon ordered Adonijah's execution, effectively squashing sibling competition to his throne.

1 Kings 3:1. *Solomon made a marriage alliance with Pharaoh king of Egypt. He took Pharaoh's daughter and brought her into the city of David* while he completed construction of the temple, his palace, and the wall surrounding Jerusalem.

This was probably the first of Solomon's many wives. It would seem that the peace with the surrounding nations during Solomon's reign was at least in part due to his multiple marriages to the daughters of the various other rulers. Solomon married her, but he didn't let her live in David's palace (**2 Chronicles 8:11**).

Solomon is best remembered for his wisdom. In the early days of his reign, he was faced with a famous case:

1 Kings 3:16–28. *Two prostitutes came to the king and stood before him. The one woman said, "Oh, my lord, this woman and I live in the same house, and I gave birth to a child while she was in the house. Then on the third day after I gave birth, this woman also gave birth. And we were alone. There was no one else with us in the house . . . And this woman's son died in the night, because she lay on him."*

That woman went on to accuse the other of switching babies in the middle of the night, saying she didn't discover the change until the next morning. The second woman insisted that what happened was just the opposite—that the living child was hers.

Solomon solved the problem and discovered the true mother of the child by ordering that the living baby be split in two, with half given to each woman. The real mother surrendered her claim in order to save her son, upon which Solomon gave her the child, identifying the little boy as hers.

It's interesting that, in the midst of ruling the country, problems of state and his supervision of building the temple, Solomon took time from his busy schedule to listen to two prostitutes, probably considered the very lowest of society. He treated them as valuable human beings, just like the Lord deals with us and as we also should regard each other, no matter what our failures and shortcomings. And he answered their request in a way that was best for all concerned.

Another famous incident from Solomon's reign was the visit by the queen of Sheba. **1 Kings 10:1–13** and **2 Chronicles 9:1–12** are almost carbon copy accounts of her stay. Both references also mention *King Solomon gave to the queen of Sheba all that she desired, whatever she asked.*

Was the queen of Sheba from Ethiopia, Yemen, or Egypt? *Biblical Archaeology Society*[25] suggests that Sheba is present-day Ethiopia, and the queen was Makeda, whose son Menelik was also a son of Solomon. And

Encyclopedia Britannica[26] lists the location as either Arabia or Ethiopia and repeats the claim that she was pregnant when she left Jerusalem. Was the queen of Sheba the object of the **Song of Solomon?** Perhaps, but we're not there yet.

1 Kings 11:1–3. *King Solomon loved many foreign women, along with the daughter of Pharaoh . . . from the nations concerning which the LORD had said to the people of Israel, "You shall not enter into marriage with them, neither shall they with you, for surely they will turn away your heart after their gods." Solomon clung to these in love. He had 700 wives, who were princesses, and 300 concubines. And his wives turned away his heart.*

It had started with Pharaoh's daughter, whom Solomon married as possibly a political move—a practice observed by monarchs in other times and places. Solomon, however, carried his sexual diplomacy to the extreme. He claimed 700 wives and 300 concubines! Good grief!

1 Kings 11:4–8. *When Solomon was old his wives turned away his heart after other gods, and his heart was not wholly true to the LORD his God, as was the heart of David his father. For Solomon went after Ashtoreth the goddess of the Sidonians, and after Milcom the abomination of the Ammonites. So Solomon did what was evil in the sight of the LORD and did not wholly follow the LORD, as David his father had done. Then Solomon built a high place for Chemosh the abomination of Moab, and for Molech the abomination of the Ammonites . . . And so he did for all his foreign wives, who made offerings and sacrificed to their gods.*

Ashtoreth (in some nations called Astarte) was a fertility symbol, whose idols, often called pillars, were part of Baal worship.[27] Molech, considered by some to be the same as Milcom,[28] was a statue with a fire in his stomach, where idol worshipers sacrificed small children. Chemosh is described in *Easton's Bible Dictionary* as a "fish-god."[29]

1 Kings 11:9–11 *And the LORD was angry with Solomon, because his heart had turned away from the LORD, the God of Israel, who had appeared to him twice and had commanded him concerning this thing, that he should not go after other gods. But he did not keep what the LORD commanded. Therefore* *the LORD said to Solomon, "Since this has been your practice and you have not kept my covenant and my statutes that I have commanded you, I will surely tear the kingdom from you and will give it to your servant."*

Solomon had sanctioned and encouraged the worship of those statues, many of which were pornographic. In the end, he had actually also worshiped them himself. Therefore, the whole nation became permanently divided shortly after his death. In keeping with His promise to David, God saw to it that the tribe of Judah and most of the Levites remained in the southern nation, which kept their allegiance to David's descendants. Their pedigrees traced back through King David, but many of those southern rulers were just as bad as their northern neighbors. Even there, those same idols remained as a temptation, sometimes worshiped, sometimes removed, and sometimes even burned and ground to powder. They always popped up again, until finally, the Lord allowed first the Northern Kingdom and then even Judah to be totally exiled from the land.

JEROBOAM I (NORTHERN KINGDOM)

1 Kings 11:29–40 and **12:25–33.** Jeroboam was the one who was actually chosen by God to take charge of the northern portion of the newly divided kingdom. A large percentage of those tribes were tired of all the taxes and of working on Solomon's building projects, so they didn't take kindly to Solomon's son, Rehoboam, when he bragged that he would be even more dictatorial. Although there was no civil war at the time of division, there was constant animosity between the kingdoms as long as they both existed.

Jeroboam did not worship pornographic idols, but he did something just as bad. Instead, he built an entire religion around two golden calves, reminiscent of what happened when Moses was on Mount Sinai receiving the Ten Commandments. In the following decades, the Baals and Ashtoreths would again appear in that nation, crowding out the true God in people's hearts and minds.

When Jeroboam walked off with the ten northern tribes, many of the faithful pulled up stakes and migrated to the Southern Kingdom. Most of the farmers knew they would not be able to obtain ground in the south because of the tribal boundaries that were established when the land was first settled. Many chose to remain in the north and hoped they would still be allowed to worship across the border in the newly built temple in Jerusalem. The majority, perhaps, just went with the flow and accepted the new regime, both politically and theologically.

REHOBOAM (SOUTHERN KINGDOM)

2 Chronicles 12:13–14. Rehoboam, son of Solomon and an Ammonite woman named Naamah, was crowned at forty-one and reigned seventeen years. *He did evil, for he did not set his heart to seek the Lord.*

Rehoboam didn't learn from his mistakes or those of his father Solomon. His mother, an Ammonite by birth, probably worshiped Molech, the idol that received child sacrifices.

1 Kings 14:22–24. *Judah did what was evil in the sight of the Lord, and they provoked him to jealousy with their sins that they committed, more than all that their fathers had done. For they also built for themselves high places and pillars and Asherim on every high hill and under every green tree, and there were also male cult prostitutes in the land. They did according to all the abominations of the nations that the Lord drove out before the people of Israel.*

It just went downhill from there. The people followed Rehoboam's lead, even as he continued in Solomon's bad practices. They made pornographic *sacred pillars* and *Asherah posts* (**2 Kings 17:10** Beck), then worshiped them with cult prostitution, both male and female. Because of their growing immorality, God allowed the Egyptians to capture large portions of their territory and to remove all the golden shields from the temple built in Solomon's era. Before Rehoboam's life and reign ended, he had eighteen wives and sixty concubines (**2 Chronicles 11:21**).

ABIJAH (SOUTHERN KINGDOM)

2 Chronicles 13:1–2, 21 and **1 Kings 15:3.** Next was Abijah, son of King Rehoboam and Maacah from Gibeah, a granddaughter of Absalom. *He walked in all the sins that his father did before him.* Abijah was so bad that the Lord only allowed him three years to rule. We also know he had fourteen wives, twenty-two sons, and sixteen daughters.

ASA (SOUTHERN KINGDOM)

1 Kings 15:9–14. Asa, a son of King Abijah, reigned for forty-one years. Good King Asa *put away the male cult prostitutes out of the land and removed all the idols that his fathers had made. He also removed Maacah his mother from being queen mother because she had made an abominable image for Asherah. And Asa cut down her image and burned it at the brook Kidron. But the high places were not taken away. Nevertheless, the heart of Asa was wholly true to the LORD all his days.* **2 Chronicles 15:16–17** repeats much of this passage verbatim.

2 Chronicles 14:2–5. *Asa . . . took away the foreign altars and the high places and broke down the pillars and cut down the Asherim and commanded Judah to seek the LORD, the God of their fathers, and to keep the law and the commandment. He also took out of all the cities of Judah the high places and the incense altars. And the kingdom had rest under him.*

At last! A good king! A ruler who not only believed in and worshiped the God of Abraham, Isaac, and Jacob but who also made sure to remove the various idols from areas under his jurisdiction. Beck clarifies the apparent contradiction in the final sentences this way:

1 Kings 15:14. *Although the pagan hill shrines were not torn down, Asa was at heart loyal to the LORD all his life.*

2 Chronicles 14:5. *From all the cities of Judah he put away the high places and the altars for incense. And with him the kingdom had peace.*

It sounds like Asa made sure the towns in the Southern Kingdom were purged of idols, but the shrines scattered across the countryside remained. He even went north of the border to get rid of some abominable statues, although he wasn't able to do a full purging in those areas. In any case, the cleanup project must have been major. Asa led his citizens to be faithful to the God of their fathers, and his nation had peace for thirty-five years.

OMRI (NORTHERN KINGDOM)

Meanwhile, in the Northern Kingdom, conditions were going from bad to worse. As that break-away nation continued its downward trek into idolatry/pornography, one king would often be dethroned when someone from the military killed him and took over as ruler. Then the new monarch would be assassinated by another leader—sometimes after only reigning a few days. Occasionally, but rarely, a son would get to follow his father as king.

1 Kings 16:25–26. *Omri did what was evil in the sight of the LORD, and did more evil than all who were before him. For he walked in all the way of Jeroboam the son of Nebat, and in the sins that he made Israel to sin, provoking the LORD, the God of Israel, to anger by their idols.*

The major political change brought about during Omri's time was a relocation of the Northern capital to a hilltop he called Samaria, where he built a heavily fortified city. Except for that, it was business as usual without reference to God in what was becoming an increasingly pagan nation.

AHAB, JEZEBEL, AND THE PROPHET ELIJAH (NORTHERN KINGDOM)

1 Kings 16:29–33. Late in Asa's reign in Judah, Omri's son Ahab began his twenty-two-year reign in the Northern Kingdom. *Ahab the son of Omri did evil in the sight of the LORD.* Not only did Ahab embrace the religion invented by Jereboam, the first northern king, . . . *he took for his wife Jezebel the daughter of Ethbaal king of the Sidonians, and went and served Baal and worshiped him. He erected an altar for Baal in the house of Baal, which he built in Samaria. And Ahab made an Asherah. Ahab did more to provoke the LORD, the God of Israel, to anger than all the kings of Israel who were before him.*

These two were so bad that they were famous for their behavior. The *Merriam-Webster* dictionary gives the historical biblical Jezebel as its first meaning of her name, but its second is "often not capitalized: an impudent, shameless, or morally unrestrained woman."[30] In other words, she wasn't even remotely nice.

1 Kings 17. Those were also the days of Elijah the prophet, who warned both Ahab and his people that their wicked ways would bring God's wrath upon the entire nation. Ahab, and especially Jezebel, refused to listen to Elijah and, in fact, actively sought to kill him. Finally, Elijah delivered God's warning that for the next three years, there would be a drought so bad that not even dew would fall. Once the message was delivered, Elijah made a hasty escape to avoid capture and certain execution.

From this, we get the famous account of the ravens (crows) who brought Elijah sandwiches twice a day while he hid out by a small stream. When that source of water dried up, Elijah was told to go north, out of the country, where because of his presence in a widowed single mother's household, the Lord provided her with food for as long as the famine lasted. During that time, the woman's young boy died, but Elijah's prayers revived him.

1 Kings 18. Finally, after the three years had expired, God sent Elijah back to Samaria with a message for Ahab. It was time for a showdown between God's faithful spokesman and the 450 prophets of Baal that Jezebel had on the government payroll. So Elijah challenged them to a contest to prove which deity was willing and able to answer the supplications of his worshipers. The odds appeared to be 450 to one, but those priests of Baal couldn't even produce smoke from their offering. Meanwhile, Elijah prepared a similar setup of rocks, wood, and slaughtered animal. To top it off, he dug a trench and poured twelve huge jars of water over his sacrifice. Then he prayed and God answered with fire from heaven that even consumed the rocks.

Finally, the people could see the contrast. They surrounded and killed all 450 of Baal's prophets. The Lord replied with rain, ending the drought.

The people had repented, but the rulers were still alive and furious. In the midst of the downpour, Elijah once more ran for his life. God called him from there to anoint Elisha as his successor and Jehu to be king of Israel.

2 Kings 9:30–37. Years later, when Jehu deposed Ahab's son from the throne, Jezebel was still living in the palace. As she leaned out of an upper window to taunt the new monarch, two of her servants pushed Jezebel out into the path of the victorious cavalry. Trampled by the horses and pulled apart by dogs, most of Jezebel's body had totally disappeared by the time someone sought to bury her remains. She was one very evil lady.

1 Kings 21:25–26. *(There was none who sold himself to do what was evil in the sight of the LORD like Ahab, whom Jezebel his wife incited. He acted very abominably in going after idols, as the Amorites had done, whom the LORD cast out before the people of Israel.)*

Nobody would want this written on his or her tombstone.

JEHOSHAPHAT (SOUTHERN KINGDOM)

1 Kings 22:41–46. Jehoshaphat, son of King Asa and Azubah (probably a native Hebrew) was crowned at age thirty-five and reigned for twenty-five years. *He walked in all the way of Asa his father. He did not turn aside from it, doing what was right in the sight of the LORD. Yet the high places were not taken away, and the people still sacrificed and made offerings on the high places. Jehoshaphat also made peace with the king of Israel . . . And from the land he exterminated the remnant of the male cult prostitutes who remained in the days of his father Asa.*

2 Chronicles 17:6. *His heart was courageous in the ways of the LORD. And furthermore, he took the high places and the Asherim out of Judah.*

For a possible explanation of the apparent discrepancy between the above passages, see my theory about a similar wording in the history of Jehoshaphat's father, King Asa. While Asa's reforms had been nationwide, there were still pockets of resistance remaining. Jehoshaphat destroyed more pornographic idols and closed the male prostitution establishments. Because he did these things, the Lord gave the country of Judah twenty-five years of peace and prosperity in contrast to the drought plaguing the tribes north of the border.

THE PROPHET ELISHA (NORTHERN KINGDOM)

2 Kings 2:19–22. Elijah had gone to heaven in a fiery chariot. Elisha had taken up his mantle as a prophet to the Northern Kingdom. Soon after the changeover, the residents of one of the northern cities complained to Elisha that their water was polluted. He cured their problem by throwing salt into the spring that supplied the community. The miracle was not so much in what was done for a cure as in the fact that one jar of salt took care of the difficulty permanently. Indeed, God's promise through Elisha was interesting: *"I have healed this water; from now on neither death nor miscarriage shall come from it."*

JORAM, SON OF AHAB (NORTHERN KINGDOM)

At this point, these two kingdoms and their monarchs become very confusing. Bible Gateway[31] gives us fifty-two English translations of **2 Kings 8:16**, the verse that lists both of the kings who followed Ahab and Jehoshaphat to their respective thrones. Most of those translations tell us that *Joram the son of Ahab* ruled in Israel, the Northern Kingdom. Then they tell us that *Jehoram son of Jehoshaphat* reigned in Judah, the Southern Kingdom. Eight of those translations invert the order of those statements, but an additional two[32] translations call them BOTH *Joram*. And Beck uses the names interchangeably. In any case, the one in Israel was a son of Ahab and Jezebel. The one in Judah was married to a daughter of Ahab and Jezebel. They were in-laws. With that kind of family ties, we would expect all sorts of bad activity.

2 Kings 3:1–3. When Ahab and Jezebel's son inherited the throne of the Northern Kingdom, *He put away the pillar of Baal that his father had made,* but he apparently let all the rest of the pornography and attendant idol worship remain. He was graded as evil, but not quite as bad as his parents.

2 Kings 6:24–31. It is possible that during his reign Ben-hadad, king of Aram[33] besieged the capital of Samaria. In the resulting famine, conditions were so desperate that women were cooking and eating children—their own or each other's. Good grief!

2 Kings 8:7–15. That same Ben-hadad was killed by Hazael, who then took over the nation of Aram. About his reign, Elisha prophesied, *"I know the evil that you will do to the people of Israel. You will . . . dash in pieces their little ones and rip open their pregnant women."*

He was not a nice guy.

JEHORAM, SON-IN-LAW OF AHAB (SOUTHERN KINGDOM)

Now back to Judah, where Jehoshaphat's son was king for only eight years:

2 Chronicles 21:4–6. We are told he *killed all his brothers with the sword, and also some of the princes of Israel . . . And he walked in the way of the kings of Israel, as the house of Ahab had done, for the daughter of Ahab was his wife. And he did what was evil in the sight of the* LORD.

That this son of Jehoshaphat was married to a daughter of Ahab and Jezebel was probably a political decision by his father, but it was indeed a very bad choice. Following the lead of his in-laws, he was a very bad king.

AHAZIAH (SOUTHERN KINGDOM)

2 Chronicles 22:2–4. Ahaziah, son of King Jehoram and Ahab and Jezebel's daughter Athaliah, was twenty-two when he was crowned, only to reign for a single year. *He also walked in the ways of the house of Ahab, for his mother was his counselor in doing wickedly. He did what was evil in the sight of the* LORD, *as the house of Ahab had done. For after the death of his father they were his counselors, to his undoing.*

To top that off, when Ahaziah was killed, his mother took over the throne of Judah. Her first move was to kill all Ahaziah's sons—or so she thought.

JEHU (NORTHERN KINGDOM)

2 Kings 10. Meanwhile, up in the Northern Kingdom, a military leader named Jehu had just killed Ahab's family and taken over the throne. One of his first acts was a sting operation in which his soldiers killed all the servants of Baal and trashed the main Baal temple in Samaria, ridding the country for a while of that idol and the prostitution which accompanied its worship. Instead of turning his people back to the Lord, however, Jehu allowed the two golden calf idols to remain.

Ezra placed this summary of the ending of the two-and-one-half trans-Jordan tribes near the beginning of his condensed history:

1 Chronicles 5:25–26. *But they broke faith with the God of their fathers, and whored after the gods of the peoples of the land, whom God had destroyed before them. So the God of Israel stirred up the spirit of Pul king of Assyria, the spirit of Tiglath-pileser king of Assyria, and he took them into exile, namely, the Reubenites, the Gadites, and the half-tribe of Manasseh, and brought them to Halah, Habor, Hara, and the river Gozan, to this day.*

Two and one-half tribes had talked Moses into letting them settle east of the Jordan River and the Sea of Galilee. During Jehu's time, those tribes were taken into exile. It is suggested they were relocated to the upper regions of the Euphrates River, in what is now eastern Turkey or northern Iraq.[34] They completely lost their identity there and disappeared from the pages of history. God is patient, but there does come a time of judgment.

JOASH (SOUTHERN KINGDOM)

2 Chronicles 24:1–3. Joash, son of King Ahaziah and Zibiah from Beersheba, took the throne when he was only seven years old. His good reign lasted forty years. *Joash did what was right in the eyes of the LORD all the days of Jehoiada the priest. Jehoiada got for him two wives, and he had sons and daughters.*

Athaliah hadn't managed to kill all the heirs to the throne after all. Apparently, King Ahaziah had had more than one wife, for Joash's mother, Zibiah, was from the very southern portion of Judah. While Zibiah may well have been killed in Athaliah's purge, one of Ahaziah's sisters—wife of

High Priest Jehoiada—had rescued this boy as a baby and managed to keep him hidden safely for six years.

Following Joash's successful coronation, his subjects tore down the temple of Baal, smashing idols and altars, and killed the priest in charge. During his reign, God's temple was cleaned and repaired, which was a major undertaking. Unfortunately, after High Priest Jehoiada died, Joash started listening to other advisors, who led him to abandon God's temple and reinstate the worship of Asherah poles and idols—and probably the prostitution that went along with them.

JEHOAHAZ (NORTHERN KINGDOM)

During the reign of Joash, a king named Jehoahaz came to power in Israel. Very little is said about him, but what we do know about him—and the citizens of his country while Jehoahaz ruled them—isn't good.

2 Kings 13:6. *They did not depart from the sins of the house of Jeroboam, which he made Israel to sin, but walked in them; and the Asherah also remained in Samaria.*

Beck even calls it a *sacred Asherah pole.*

AMAZIAH (SOUTHERN KINGDOM)

2 Chronicles 25:1–2. Amaziah, son of King Joash and a lady from Jerusalem named Jehoaddan, was crowned at twenty-five and reigned twenty-nine years. *He did what was right in the eyes of the LORD, yet not with a whole heart.*

We are told in **2 Kings 14:4** that the high places remained standing and that the people still offered sacrifices and burned incense at those locations.

Following a battle with the inhabitants of Seir,[35] Amaziah made the bad decision to bring home the idols of the nation he had conquered. He then picked a fight with the king of Israel, who took him prisoner and tore down part of the protective wall surrounding Jerusalem. Amaziah's reign ended with his assassination.

AZARIAH (ALSO CALLED UZZIAH, SOUTHERN KINGDOM)

2 Kings 15:2–4. Azariah, called Uzziah in **Chronicles**, son of King Amaziah and a Jerusalem native named Jecoliah, took the throne at age sixteen and reigned an amazing fifty-two years. *He did what was right in the eyes of the LORD, according to all that his father Amaziah had done. Nevertheless, the high places were not taken away. The people still sacrificed and made offerings on the high places.*

Azariah/Uzziah, who was a farmer at heart, had a huge army with which he overcame the Philistines and several other peoples.

2 Chronicles 26:4. *He did what was right in the eyes of the LORD, according to all that his father Amaziah had done.* Since, in both verses, he is classified as a good king, the blatant pornography of the Northern Kingdom apparently wasn't running rampant in Judah during his reign.

MENAHEM (NORTHERN KINGDOM)

2 Kings 15:16. *Menahem sacked Tiphsah and all who were in it . . . because they did not open it to him . . . and he ripped open all the women in it who were pregnant.*

He was not a nice guy. This was one of several leaders who ruled for very short periods in the Northern Kingdom as it rapidly came apart at the seams.

JOTHAM (SOUTHERN KINGDOM)

2 Kings 15:32–35. Jotham, son of King Uzziah and a Jewess named Jerusha, began his sixteen-year reign at the age of twenty-five. *He did what was right in the eyes of the LORD, according to all that his father Uzziah had done. Nevertheless, the high places were not removed. The people still sacrificed and made offerings on the high places.*

According to **2 Chronicles 27:2,** *the people still followed corrupt practices.* Again, it seems the pornographic idols, at least, weren't blatantly displayed. Jotham was counted as one of the good kings.

AHAZ (SOUTHERN KINGDOM)

2 Chronicles 28:1–4. Ahaz, son of King Jotham, was crowned at twenty and reigned for sixteen years. *He did not do what was right in the eyes of the LORD . . . but he walked in the ways of the kings of Israel. He even made metal images for the Baals, and he made offerings in the Valley of the Son of Hinnom and burned his sons as an offering, according to the abominations of the nations whom the LORD drove out before the people of Israel. And he sacrificed and made offerings on the high places and on the hills and under every green tree.*

What had been eliminated in prior generations once more reared its ugly head.

HOSHEA (NORTHERN KINGDOM)

Hoshea probably wasn't any worse than the several kings before him. The attitude of the people, however, had gone downhill until God declared,

"Enough!" He allowed the king of Assyria to conquer the entire Northern Kingdom, taking the people captive, far away from their homeland.

2 Kings 17:7–20. *This occurred because the people of Israel had sinned against the LORD their God, who had brought them up out of the land of Egypt . . . and had feared other gods and walked in the customs of the nations whom the LORD drove out before the people of Israel, and in the customs that the kings of Israel had practiced. And the people of Israel did secretly against the LORD their God things that were not right. They built for themselves high places in all their towns, from watchtower to fortified city. They set up for themselves pillars and Asherim on every high hill and under every green tree, and there they made offerings on all the high places, as the nations did whom the LORD carried away before them. And they did wicked things, provoking the LORD to anger, and they served idols, of which the LORD had said to them, "You shall not do this." Yet the LORD warned Israel and Judah by every prophet and every seer, saying, "Turn from your evil ways and keep my commandments and my statutes, in accordance with all the Law that I commanded your fathers, and that I sent to you by my servants the prophets." But they would not listen . . . They despised his statutes and his covenant that he made with their fathers and the warnings that he gave them. They went after false idols and became false, and they followed the nations that were around them, concerning whom the LORD had commanded them that they should not do like them. And they abandoned all the commandments of the LORD their God, and made for themselves metal images of two calves; and they made an Asherah and worshiped all the host of heaven and served Baal. And they burned their sons and their daughters as offerings and used divination and omens and sold themselves to do evil in the sight of the LORD, provoking him to anger. Therefore the LORD was very angry with Israel and removed them out of his sight. None was left but the tribe of Judah only. Judah also did not keep the commandments of the LORD their God, but walked in the customs that Israel had introduced. And the LORD rejected all the descendants of Israel and afflicted them and gave them into the hand of plunderers, until he had cast them out of his sight.*

2 Kings 17:24–33. The king of Assyria brought people he had captured from various other parts of his realm and settled them in the Northern Kingdom, replacing the Israelites. Those immigrants brought with them their idols and worship practices. They even tried to mingle some references to the True God into their rituals, along with their pagan customs. That was still the situation in Jesus' day, which is why observant Jews refused to travel in Samaria, if possible. Instead, they crossed the Jordan River twice to go from Galilee to Jerusalem.

HEZEKIAH (SOUTHERN KINGDOM)

2 Kings 18:1–4. Hezekiah, son of King Ahaz and probably a Jewish woman named Abijah, took the throne at twenty-five and reigned twenty-nine years. *He did what was right in the eyes of the LORD, according to all that David his father had done. He removed the high places and broke the pillars and cut down the Asherah.*

Hezekiah commanded a complete cleanup of God's temple in Jerusalem, then smashed the idols in the rest of his realm. Residents of the Northern Kingdom were deported during Hezekiah's reign, so his people ventured a bit north of the border, even cleaning out the Asherah poles, high places, and altars in great portions of that territory.

2 Kings 18:5–7. Hezekiah *trusted in the LORD, the God of Israel, so that there was none like him among all the kings of Judah after him, nor among those who were before him. For he held fast to the LORD. He did not depart from following him, but kept the commandments that the LORD commanded Moses. And the LORD was with him; wherever he went out, he prospered.*

It might have seemed like the Lord deserted Hezekiah in **2 Kings 19**, when the Assyrian king Sennacherib invaded Judah and set siege to Jerusalem, but that was really an opportunity for God to showcase His power when He killed 185,000 of the invading army in one night but left intact tents, provisions, and even animals to be appropriated by Hezekiah's people.

MANASSEH (SOUTHERN KINGDOM)

2 Kings 21:1–6. Manasseh, son of King Hezekiah and a lady named Hephzibah, was only twelve years old at his coronation. He reigned fifty-five years. *He did what was evil in the sight of the* LORD, *according to the despicable practices of the nations whom the* LORD *drove out before the people of Israel. For he rebuilt the high places that Hezekiah his father had destroyed, and he erected altars for Baal and made an Asherah, as Ahab king of Israel had done . . . And he built altars in the house of the* LORD, *of which the* LORD *had said, "In Jerusalem will I put my name." . . . And he burned his son as an offering . . . He did much evil in the sight of the* LORD, *provoking him to anger.*

I wonder if the idols in Hezekiah's time were merely removed from their shrines and temples but not chopped to pieces. It looks like Manasseh also brought in idols from the surrounding nations, and led the southern kingdom right back to the active practice of those pagan religions.

2 Kings 21:7–9. *The carved image of Asherah that he had made he set in the house of which the* LORD *said to David and to Solomon his son, "In this house, and in Jerusalem, which I have chosen out of all the tribes of Israel, I will put my name forever" . . . But they did not listen, and Manasseh led them astray to do more evil than the nations had done whom the* LORD *destroyed before the people of Israel.*

This was apparently the last straw—a pornographic idol in God's temple!

2 Kings 21:10–15. Because of all the evil Manasseh brought into his kingdom, God declared that he would bring *"upon Jerusalem and Judah such disaster that the ears of everyone who hears of it will tingle."* In fact, their punishment would be greater than that inflicted on Samaria and the Northern Kingdom.

2 Kings 21:16. Manasseh must have met some resistance to his evil actions, for we are told he *shed very much innocent blood, till he had filled Jerusalem from one end to another.*

2 Chronicles 33:10–19. God allowed the ruler of Assyria to punish Manasseh. He put him in chains, put a hook in his nose, and literally led him to Babylon by the nose. While he was there, Manasseh repented, so God led the Assyrian ruler to let Manasseh return to Jerusalem, where he removed the idols, rebuilt part of the city wall, and reinstituted worship of God. The populace kept their high places but apparently worshiped God there rather than any of the idols.

In any case, like Pandora's Box, Manasseh had opened the door to a host of evil.

AMON (SOUTHERN KINGDOM)

2 Kings 21:19–21. Amon, son of King Manasseh and a lady from Jotbah named Meshullemeth, began his two-year reign at age twenty-two. *He did what was evil in the sight of the LORD, as Manasseh his father had done. He walked in all the way in which his father walked and served the idols that his father served and worshiped them.*

Apparently, Manasseh, on his return from Babylon, hadn't completely pulverized those idols. Amon dug them back out, dusted them off, and steered his country right back toward paganism again. Thankfully, Amon was only allowed to reign for two years.

JOSIAH (SOUTHERN KINGDOM)

2 Chronicles 34:1–2. Josiah, son of King Amon and a lady from Bozkath named Jedidah, took the throne at the age of eight, reigning for thirty-one years. *He did what was right in the eyes of the LORD, and walked in the ways of David his father; and he did not turn aside to the right hand or to the left.*

We have come to the last of the good kings of Judah. Josiah was born when his father Amon was only sixteen, so the first several years of Josiah's life probably coincided with the reforms and cleanup Manasseh instituted after he was allowed to return from Babylon. Perhaps his mother, a native of Bozkath in the Judean foothills, had more influence in those early years than did his father and grandfather. Somewhere along the line, Josiah was blessed with good and godly advisors.

2 Chronicles 34:3–7. *For in the eighth year of his reign . . . he began to seek the God of David his father, and in the twelfth year he began to purge Judah and Jerusalem of the high places, the Asherim, and the carved and the metal images. And they chopped down the altars of the Baals in his presence, and he cut down the incense altars that stood above them. And he broke in pieces the Asherim and the carved and the metal images, and he made dust of them and scattered it over the graves of those who had sacrificed to them. He also burned the bones of the priests on their altars and cleansed Judah and Jerusalem. And in the cities of Manasseh, Ephraim, and Simeon, and as far as Naphtali, in their ruins all around, he broke down the altars and beat the Asherim and the images into powder and cut down all the incense altars throughout all the land of Israel.*

Josiah went far beyond the reforms of Hezekiah, totally obliterating the idols and even digging up the cemeteries around those shrines to burn the bones of those who had been priests there. It appears he might have gone as far north as Nazareth in his campaign to also clean up the areas of those former tribes.

2 Kings 22:3—23:3. In the eighteenth year of his reign, Josiah's reformers discovered a copy of *the Book of the Law*, probably Exodus through Deuteronomy. When they read God's commands aloud, Josiah was mortified. Realizing that his nation was in great danger of God's judgment for all their idolatry, Josiah called for an assembly of the entire citizenry. When those same Scriptures were read to the people, they joined Josiah in humble and complete repentance.

2 Kings 23:4–15. Then Josiah ordered the priests to clean the temple, removing *all the vessels made for Baal, for Asherah, and for all the host of heaven. He burned them outside Jerusalem in the fields of the Kidron and carried their ashes to Bethel. And he deposed the priests whom the kings of Judah had ordained to make offerings in the high places at the cities of Judah and around Jerusalem; those also who burned incense to Baal . . . And he brought out the Asherah from the house of the* LORD, *outside Jerusalem, to the brook Kidron, and burned it . . . And he broke down the houses of the male cult prostitutes who were in the house of the* LORD, *where the women wove hangings for the Asherah. And he brought all the priests out of the cities of Judah, and defiled the high places where the priests had made offerings . . . The priests of the high places did not come up to the altar of the* LORD *in Jerusalem, but they ate unleavened bread among their brothers. And he defiled Topheth . . . that no one might burn his son or his daughter as an offering to Molech . . . And the king defiled the high places . . . which Solomon the king of Israel had built for Ashtoreth the abomination of the Sidonians, and for Chemosh the abomination of Moab, and for Milcom the abomination of the Ammonites. And he broke in pieces the pillars and cut down the Asherim and filled their places with the bones of men.*

Moreover, the altar at Bethel, the high place erected by Jeroboam the son of Nebat, who made Israel to sin, that altar with the high place he pulled down and burned, reducing it to dust. He also burned the Asherah.

The amount of trash was great. The only way to do a good job of spring housecleaning was to obliterate all of it, following God's directives in **Deuteronomy 7, 12,** and **16.**

2 Kings 23:24. *Moreover, Josiah put away the mediums and the necromancers and the household gods and the idols and all the abominations that were seen in the land of Judah and in Jerusalem, that he might establish the words of the law that were written in the book that Hilkiah the priest found in the house of the* LORD.

ZEDEKIAH (SOUTHERN KINGDOM)

2 Chronicles 36:11–14. Zedekiah, son of Josiah, was twenty-one when he became king and reigned for eleven years. According to **2 Kings 24:18**, his mother was Hamutal. She is listed as a daughter of Jeremiah, but not the prophet by that name. *He did what was evil in the sight of the* LORD *his God . . . He stiffened his neck and hardened his heart against turning to the* LORD, *the God of Israel. All the officers of the priests and the people likewise were exceedingly unfaithful, following all the abominations of the nations. And they polluted the house of the* LORD *that he had made holy in Jerusalem.*

It has been said that Christianity is always just one generation removed from being wiped out in any given nation. So it was here. It didn't take long to return to all those bad habits—in spite of the warnings of several prophets. Nothing short of exile would get their attention.

2 Chronicles 36:15–16. *The* LORD, *the God of their fathers, sent persistently to them by his messengers, because he had compassion on his people and on his dwelling place. But they kept mocking the messengers of God, despising his words and scoffing at his prophets, until the wrath of the* LORD *rose against his people, until there was no remedy*

So Nebuchadnezzar deported the majority of the citizens of Judah to Babylon, where they would remain for seventy years.

6

THE BABYLONIAN ERA

EZRA, NEHEMIAH, AND Esther lived during the years the people of Judah were in exile in Babylon. Ezra and Nehemiah each led a group of returning exiles, then undertook the rebuilding of the temple and the walls of Jerusalem. Esther, as the queen of one of the Persian monarchs, was instrumental in saving Jews from annihilation.

EZRA

Since the final verses of **2 Chronicles** match almost exactly the opening verses of **Ezra**, there is speculation that he was the one who probably penned both. The dozens of lists that would almost seem to be Ezra's trademark certainly appear in each. The only issue found in **Ezra** pertinent to our study deals with the list with which his book closes.

The people of Judah had been allowed to be captured by Nebuchadnezzar because they had insisted on worshiping the pornographic idols of the surrounding nations. In many instances, in obvious opposition to God's direct commands, they had also intermarried with the natives. Those few who had been left behind, mostly the poorest members of society, had apparently not learned anything from their nation's defeat. Some of those who returned from Babylon were also involved. Just like Solomon's harem, these women had brought their religious practices with them—and quite probably their idols as well.

The temple was at least partially rebuilt. Sacrifices and even festivals had been re-established. It was time to work on the deeper problem.

Ezra 9:1–6 (Beck). Ezra was told, *"The people of Israel, including priests and Levites, have failed to separate from the people of foreign countries, from the idolatrous ways . . ."* of the local tribes and nations. *"They and their sons have married their daughters and mixed our holy race with the people of those countries, and the leaders and officials have led them in such disloyalty."*

Going beyond tearing his robe, the traditional sign of mourning, Ezra even started pulling out his hair. As he *sat down dazed,* a crowd was gathering, comprised of *all who trembled at the words of the God of Israel against this great disloyalty of the returned exiles.*

As the day ended, Ezra knelt and prayed, *"My God . . . I feel ashamed and blush to look up to You, my God; our sins are so many they overwhelm us, and our guilt is so great it reaches heaven."* Ezra was obviously upset.

This is why there's a problem with mixed marriages:

For my parents' generation, the wedding of a Baptist and a Lutheran would have been considered a mixed marriage. What usually happened next, at least in small-town America, was that one of the spouses would join the other's church, where they would actively attend and participate as a family. One or the other set of grandparents might have had occasional problems with that arrangement, but they would be happy that their grandchildren were being raised as Christians. That's not a return to idolatry.

Two generations later, the term "mixed marriage" would only be understood as having racial connotations. While my children's generation would not use the same terminology, however, they probably would agree that the wedding of a Christian and a Buddhist could lead to some rough moments.

So what does God have to say on the subject? What is His definition of a mixed marriage, and what are His reasons for that outlook?

Of the natives living in the land the Hebrews were to take over, God said,

Deuteronomy 7:3–4 (Beck). *"Don't intermarry with them: don't let your daughter marry his son or your son marry his daughter, because they will turn your sons away from Me to serve other gods. Then the LORD will get very angry with you and quickly destroy you."*

Exodus 34:15–16 (Beck). If they ignored God's injunction and intermarried anyway, *"When their daughters lust after their gods, they'll lead your sons to lust after them too."*

Look around you some Sunday morning, whether you are inside a church or somewhere else. Do you see any couples in which a Christian married a non-Christian? In what percentage of the marriages does it look like God was correct in His prediction? What is the effect on the following generation?

Review again the experiences of Solomon in **1 Kings 11** for a rather graphic example of what can happen in those instances. It can indeed be tragic.

Ezra 9:7–9 is an admission that, because of the sins of previous generations, the exile to Babylon had been a deserved punishment. In fact, the amazing thing was that God hadn't just wiped them off the face of the earth and started over with another people group. Instead, when they, as refugees in a foreign land, had turned again to God, He moved the pagan Persian rulers to allow and even encourage them to return to their homeland.

But the few Jewish citizens who had been left behind in the land also needed to abandon all the ways in which they were still flagrantly breaking God's laws. Going forward, in order for everyone to become one nation under God, they had to make some lifestyle changes.

Ezra's prayer continues:

Ezra 9:10–15 (Beck). *"We have forsaken Your commandments . . ."* just like Moses and the prophets had warned them, *". . . The country you are going to take is polluted due to its polluted people, whose idolatrous practices have filled it from one end to another with uncleanness. And now, don't let your daughters marry their sons or your sons marry their daughters, and don't seek their peace and prosperity; then you will be strong and eat the good things the land produces, and this land will be an inheritance for you and* *your descendants forever.' After all that has happened to us for the wicked things we did and for our great guilt—seeing that You, our God, have punished us less than we deserve and have now given us some survivors—if we should again break your commandments and intermarry with these idolatrous people, won't You be even more angry with us till You have consumed us and there are no survivors left?"*

The people responded, resolved to fix the problem:

Ezra 10:1–5 (Beck). *While Ezra prayed and confessed, weeping and bowing down before God's temple, a great assembly of men, women, and children of Israel gathered to him, and the people wept bitterly . . . "We have been disloyal to our God and have taken foreign wives into our homes from the people of this country; but now there is some hope for Israel in this matter. So let us now make a covenant with our God to put away all such women and the children born of them. . . just as the Law tells us."*

So Ezra stood up *and had the leaders, priests, Levites, and all the rest of Israel swear to do what they had said.*

Ezra 10:6–9. The very next morning, a proclamation was issued calling everyone to assemble in Jerusalem three days later. Failure to appear would result in loss of property, with that person becoming once more an outcast.

So they came, both men and women, and assembled in the area in front of the temple in spite of a heavy downpour, as Ezra laid out the problem:

Ezra 10:10–11 (Beck). *"You have been disloyal and brought foreign wives into your homes and so added to Israel's guilt. And now, confess to the LORD, the God of your fathers, and do what He wants; separate from the people of this country and from the foreign wives."*

God is not normally in favor of divorce. In this case, it must have been the lesser of two evils.

Ezra 10:12–14 (Beck). *Then the whole assembly promised loudly, "So be it. We must do as you say . . . Let all who in our towns have taken home foreign wives come, each at a time appointed for him, and with them let the elders and judges of each town come, till the blazing anger of our God is turned away from us in this matter."*

Ezra 10:15–44 (Beck). Apparently, only four of the local leaders opposed that plan. Ezra selected clan and family heads, who, in three months, compiled a listing of 112 men who had foreign wives, including at least four of the priests. It seems that all 112 *put away their wives*, possibly sending the children of those divorces out of their homes (and perhaps communities) as well.

NEHEMIAH

Nehemiah 8:1–12. Nehemiah, governor and military leader, gives us the rest of the story. The people, this time including women and children, gathered some months later in Jerusalem. They stood for an entire morning while Ezra read aloud the Laws of Moses. Then the Levites, assistants to the priests, divided them into smaller groups to explain what had been read.

Nehemiah 9 and **10.** Later still, the people once more assembled, this time with prayer and fasting. Following a long prayer of repentance, they signed an oath to obey God's laws, as given through Moses. Among other things, they vowed:

Nehemiah 10:30 (Beck). *"We will not have our daughters marry the people of the country or have their daughters marry our sons."*

They rebuilt the wall around Jerusalem, providing protection from the foreigners who had taken over much of the territory in the absence of the Jews. When that task was completed, they declared another festival to dedicate that wall. The day started with a grand processional and worship service and continued with more Bible study.

Nehemiah 13:1–3 (Beck). *On that day the Book of Moses was read while the people were listening, and there it was found to be written that nobody from Ammon or Moab should ever get into God's congregation, because they didn't come to the Israelites with food and water but hired Balaam against them to curse them. But our God turned the curse into a blessing. When the people heard the Law, they put away from Israel everyone of mixed race.*

This purging quite possibly reached to include all members of those nationalities living in the country—servants, merchants, and spouses.

Nehemiah 13:23–27 (Beck). *In those days I also saw the Jews who had married women from Ashdod, Ammon, and Moab. Half their children spoke the language of Ashdod; they couldn't understand Hebrew well enough to speak it, but spoke the languages of each people.*

So I argued with them, cursing them, striking some of them, pulling out their hair; and I made them swear by God: "We won't give our daughters in marriage to their sons, and we won't take their daughters for our sons or ourselves." I said, "Didn't Solomon king of Israel sin in this way? Among many nations there wasn't a king like him. God loved him, and God made him king of all Israel. But those foreign women were the reason for his sin. Must we hear the same about you, that you too do all this great wrong and turn disloyal to our God by taking foreign wives into your homes?"

Nehemiah could have taken that history lesson back to the days preceding the flood, the days when *the sons of God saw how beautiful the daughters of man were, and they married the women they liked best* (**Genesis 6:2** Beck). All the way from that century on, through Solomon's dynasty, and even today, while the believing spouse may continue worshiping God, how often we see, in a mixed marriage, that their children are more haphazard in their church attendance and totally abandon Bible reading and study. Then this problem compounds with the third generation and soon, a whole nation has forgotten about God.

That explains why the Lord was so adamant about not marrying foreign women. That these non-Israelite spouses probably brought their pornographic idols and worship-by-prostitution into the marriage would have definitely compounded the problem.

Nehemiah's purge may not be a duplicate account of Ezra's. Nehemiah mentions only one man, just giving his family lineage. Ezra, by contrast, only gave first names. So there may have been one purge or two, with this referring to a later group, possibly as more people moved into Jerusalem from the surrounding villages or came back from Babylon.

Nehemiah 13:28–29 (Beck). Nehemiah's reaction was as strong as Ezra's, including this about the grandson of the high priest, who had married a daughter of Sanballat, the local leader of the opposition to Nehemiah and all the repairs the returning exiles were accomplishing: *I chased him away from me. Remember them, my God, because they have polluted the priesthood and the covenant of the priests and Levites.*

ESTHER

Esther, one of the Jewish girls either taken from Judah to Babylon in the final deportation or born soon after arrival, was raised by her Uncle Mordecai because her parents were deceased. King Xerxes of the book of **Esther** ruled from 486 to 465 BC, so these events happened in that time frame.[36]

Esther 1:1–9. Probably following a major military conquest, Xerxes hosted a banquet to brag about his victory. That the feast was supposed to last 180 days gives us some indication of the importance of the nation that had been conquered. That extravaganza was for the men. Queen Vashti gave a similar feast for the women of the court.

Esther 1:10–12. Seven days into those feasts, when King Xerxes was becoming perhaps a bit tipsy, he sent seven of his servants to command Queen Vashti to appear at his banquet so he could show off her great beauty. She refused, making the king furious.

Esther 1:15. Turning to his advisors (probably early members of the same group of Wise Men we find in **Matthew**), Xerxes requested a punishment sufficient to impress all his subjects that no one, not even the queen, was allowed to refuse an order from the king.

Esther 1:16–22. Realizing that, once word got out that Queen Vashti had rejected an order from King Xerxes, other men also might no longer be able to rule the roost in their own households, those sages were quick to suggest that the queen be deposed and forbidden to ever again approach the king. In fact, they requested that a royal order be sent to all provinces, in their native languages, to decree that each man should be master of his household.

Esther 2:1–4 (Beck). But, of course, that would leave a vacuum. The solution proposed by the younger cabinet members was to call for a kingdom-wide beauty contest. The call went out, saying *all the beautiful virgin girls in the entire kingdom* should be brought to a harem so that the king could choose a new queen from among their number.

Gentlemen, for some of you, the thought of having a harem of beautiful maidens at your beck and call might sound very attractive. I assure you, for at least some women, the idea of being part of that grouping has all the attraction of employing someone else's toothbrush—after they've used it to clean the bathroom floor. Just because something is common practice in a culture doesn't make it right.

Esther 2:5–11 (Beck). Esther, who *had a fine figure and was beautiful,* was chosen. While it was her beauty that brought her to that position, it was her character that earned the attention of the eunuch in charge of that harem, who then gave her special attention and advice. Meanwhile, Esther kept her Jewish heritage secret.

We haven't run into the term *eunuch* very often thus far, but they play a large role in this story. Both the *Encyclopedia Britannica* and *Merriam-Webster* dictionary define eunuch as "a castrated man." Among other things, eunuchs, having no testosterone, were considered safe as servants of the king, and especially to work with the women of court and the harem.[37]

Esther 2:12–14 (Beck). Apparently, in spite of having picked the most beautiful virgins in the land, the Persians believed their beauty had to be enhanced with *6 months with oil of myrrh and 6 months with perfumes and other ointments* [sic]. At the end of those twelve months, each young woman was taken to the king's bedchamber, then, after spending the night, she was moved from there to a second harem that was overseen by a different eunuch. *She didn't go to the king again unless the king liked her and called her by name.*

Esther 2:15–18 (Beck). Esther impressed the king. In fact, *the king loved Esther more than all the other women, and he was much kinder to her than to all the other virgins.* Xerxes crowned Esther as his new queen. He was so happy that he gave another big feast—even going so far as to cut taxes and give away generous gifts.

Esther 2:19–20. Xerxes had his queen, but that didn't satisfy him. We're told that a second collection of virgins was made. We also know that, although her heritage remained unknown, Uncle Mordecai had devised a way to keep in touch with Esther through the maids and eunuchs who had been assigned to her.

Esther 3 and **4.** Then came the crisis. Haman, one of the chief officers in Xerxes' government, insisted on being treated as "almost royalty," but Mordecai refused to bow down to him. Haman, therefore, devised a scheme whereby he could kill not only Mordecai but all the Jews and make it look like he was doing a favor for the king.

In response, Mordecai dressed in sackcloth and ashes—the traditional mourning garb of the Jews—and again took up his listening spot near Esther's harem. In fact, it almost seems like he was trying to send her an announcement: "There's a big problem. Dispatch one of your servants. I have a message for you!"

Esther 4:10–11 (Beck). Esther directed one of her servants to give Mordecai this message: *"All the king's men and the people in the king's provinces know that if any man or woman goes to the king in the inner court without being called, there is only one verdict for him—death—unless the king holds out to him the golden scepter to let him live; and I haven't been called to come to the king for 30 days now"* [sic].

We can almost hear Esther thinking, "Xerxes has all these new women to play with, so he's forgotten that he once thought I was special. Uncle Mordecai, I don't think I have any influence at court anymore."

Esther 4:13–14 (Beck). Mordecai's reply was short and to the point, *"Don't think that you of all the Jews will escape in the king's palace. If you are silent now, relief and rescue will come to the Jews from somewhere else, but* *you and your father's family will perish. Who knows, perhaps you became queen for such a time as this."*

Esther 4:15–17 (Beck). Esther accepted her assignment, but she asked for help. In fact, she knew the results could be disastrous without divine protection and guidance. She requested all the Jews in the whole capital city to declare a complete fast for the next three days, not eating or drinking anything, and to spend that entire time praying for her and the success of her mission. She and her servants would do the same. Only then would she *"go to the king, even if it is against the law. If I perish, I perish."*

Esther 5:1–2 (Beck). Esther, wearing all the royal finery of her position as queen, entered Xerxes' throne room three days later. God, who is in charge of men and nations, brought to the king's mind just how delightful this queen was. King Xerxes *held out to Esther the golden scepter in his hand,* and she was safely granted an audience with the king.

Esther 5:3–5. Xerxes was so delighted to see his queen again that he offered to give her whatever she desired, up to half his kingdom. But all that Esther requested was that Xerxes and Haman come to a banquet she had prepared for them.

Esther 5:6–8. Again, after feasting, Xerxes asked Esther what he could do for her. In answer, she invited both of them to another banquet the following night.

Esther 7:1–6 (Beck). The following evening, escorted by the king's eunuchs, Xerxes and Haman went to dine at Esther's apartment. Once the meal was ended, the king again asked Esther what the problem was and what he could decree to solve it.

Then Esther revealed that she was a Jew and that her entire nation was slated for extermination according to the decree into which Haman had talked the king. Then *Haman was terrified as he faced the king and the queen.*

Esther 7:7–8 (Beck). *Angrily the king got up from drinking wine and went into the palace garden. But Haman stayed to beg Queen Esther for his life . . . When the king came back from the palace garden into the palace* *where they'd been drinking wine, Haman was lying on the couch where Esther was.* "Is he even going to rape the queen in my presence, here in the palace?" Xerxes fumed.

Instead of sitting at tables, as we do, in that culture, the rich and powerful reclined on couches to eat. Xerxes' reaction, after blowing off steam in the palace garden, would seem to indicate that Haman wasn't keeping his hands to himself, thus, adding insult to injury.

It was the eunuchs who told the king about the seventy-five-foot-high gallows Haman had erected at his estate, intending to hang Mordecai when the Jew-extermination edict was carried out. Immediately, Haman's head was covered with a sack, then he was taken home where, high above the ground so the whole community could see, he was hanged from the neck until dead.

Esther 8, 9, and **10** (Beck). That edict to kill the Jews was still on the books. Calling Mordecai into consultation, Xerxes now decreed that the Jews were to be allowed to defend themselves, and in fact, had the king's permission to kill or destroy all who would come against them, and even to confiscate their property. That new law went out to all the officials *of the 127 provinces from India to Ethiopia, to each province in its own writing and to each people in their own language, and to the Jews in their writing and their language.*

The Feast of Purim today still commemorates that event.

Ezra, Nehemiah, and **Esther** are grouped together by their timing during the Babylonian exile and are also tied together by the common thread of mixed marriages.

We don't know if any of the non-Jews involved ever came to faith in the God of Abraham, Isaac, and Jacob. We don't know whether or how many of those born as Hebrews kept their faith. We don't know anything about the impact on their children.

What we do know is that God can take that sort of arrangement and use it for His purpose and for the good of His people. May He continue to do so, for we are indeed a nation of mixed marriages.

7

NEITHER HEBREW HISTORY
NOR PROPHECY

SANDWICHED BETWEEN THE end of **Esther** and the beginning of **Isaiah** are five units commonly called "Wisdom Literature." A lot of this is poetry—not rhyming verses, as in English poems, but Hebrew poetry, with each part of the two-line couplet (or occasionally three-line triplet) saying almost the same thing or else further developing the thought, but using different words. Keep that structural concept in mind as we study those verses that apply to our topic.

JOB

The Bible doesn't tell us who wrote the book of Job. We can determine from the environmental descriptions that Job lived during or immediately following the Ice Age that would have occurred in the early centuries following the flood. That means Job was a contemporary of Abraham, although they may not have known each other. The first mention of Job outside the book that bears his name comes from the time of the Babylonian exile, in **Ezekiel 14:14** and **20**. In the New Testament, **James 5:11** also speaks of him.

Here's what happened: Job, a faithful believer in the God of Noah, was blessed with a large and prosperous family, plus sheep, goats, camels, oxen, donkeys, and the servants to take care of those thousands of animals. Satan, who was mean and nasty as always, talked God into letting him kill Job's children and servants and either kill or steal all his livestock. While Job mourned the loss of his sons and daughters, he still maintained his faith in God.

Then Satan got God's permission to inflict Job with *loathsome sores*, head to toe (**Job 2:4–8**), a malady that sounds a lot like a really bad case of chickenpox or shingles. Still, Job believed and refused to blame God for the disasters that had befallen him.

Word got out that Job was experiencing a catastrophe. Three of his friends decided to pay him a visit, but they were so shocked at his appearance that, at first, they couldn't find a thing to say. Job opens the conversation.

Job 3:2–4. *Job said: "Let the day perish on which I was born, and the night that said, 'A man is conceived.'"*

Job 3:11. *"Why did I not die at birth, come out from the womb and expire?"*

Notice that, while Job wishes he had never been conceived, let alone born, he does not blame God for his present predicament, nor does he (at this point) demand an explanation as to why all that grief had come his way. He also claimed "personhood" from the moment of conception.

Following haranguing discourses from all Job's friends and Job's denials of having done the sins of which they accuse him, Job brings forth that question we so often ask: "Why, God?" Please note also that Job refers to himself in those days after conception as "me," not "the fetus that became me."

Several chapters follow in which Job and his "friends" almost fling statements at each other. His friends are certain Job must be a horrible fellow, although they apparently weren't aware of his misdeeds before. One statement in those chapters has words that are pertinent to our study.

Job 24:15–16. *"The eye of the adulterer also waits for the twilight, saying, 'No eye will see me'; and he veils his face. In the dark they dig through houses; by day they shut themselves up; they do not know the light."*

Those words are part of Job's long list of criminals and other evildoers. The crimes go all the way from moving landmarks (thus, stealing real estate) and robbing the poor—rather than assisting them—to murder and other mayhem.

Starting with **Job 26,** Job makes a very long statement in his defense. Remembering that he is a married man, Job declares that he has also kept his mind from lustful thoughts.

Job 31:1–2. *"I have made a covenant with my eyes; how then could I gaze at a virgin? What would be my portion from God above and my heritage from the Almighty on high?"*

He goes on to say that if he had ever coveted his neighbor's wife, he would deserve more problems than he already had.

Job 31:9–12. *"If my heart has been enticed toward a woman, and I have lain in wait at my neighbor's door, then let my wife grind for another, and let others bow down on her. For that would be a heinous crime; that would be an iniquity to be punished by the judges; for that would be a fire that consumes."*

When Job stopped to take a breath, Elihu jumped into the discussion to remind them that God has a variety of ways in which He can punish the wicked.

Job 36:13–14. *"The godless in heart cherish anger . . . They die in youth, and their life ends among the cult prostitutes."*

Even at this early point in human history, worship of other gods apparently often included cult prostitution.

The book closes with the Lord reminding Job that the Creator is so much wiser than human beings that there is no way whatsoever that people, even believers, will be able to second guess why God does what He does. God then chews out Job's friends for telling lies about Job and gives him back double portions of everything the devil had taken away.

PSALMS

The **Psalms** were the Hebrew's hymns. Many were written by David, both before and after he became king. Other authors range from Moses to musicians assigned to sing in the temple that was built by Solomon to some of those exiled to Babylon. Authorship of many psalms had been lost by the time the Old Testament canon was closed.

In addition, many of these songs have lines that are prophetic about the earthly life and ministry of the coming Messiah, who we know to be Jesus, but the authors certainly didn't have that whole picture at the time.

PSALM 45

Psalm 45:1–15. *My heart overflows with a pleasing theme; I address my verses to the king . . . You are the most handsome of the sons of men; grace is poured upon your lips; therefore God has blessed you forever . . . Your throne, O God, is forever and ever. The scepter of your kingdom is a scepter of uprightness; you have loved righteousness and hated wickedness. Therefore God, your God, has anointed you with the oil of gladness beyond your companions; your robes are all fragrant with myrrh and aloes and cassia. From ivory palaces stringed instruments make you glad; daughters of kings are among your ladies of honor; at your right hand stands the queen in gold of Ophir. Hear, O daughter, and consider, and incline your ear: forget your people and your father's house, and the king will desire your beauty. Since he is your lord, bow to him . . . All glorious is the princess in her chamber, with robes interwoven with gold. In many-colored robes she is led to the king, with her virgin companions following behind her. With joy and gladness they are led along as they enter the palace of the king.*

Psalm 45 is identified as "a Maskil of the Sons of Korah; a love song."

Since the only gentlemen named Korah who appear in the historical books of the Old Testament were probably deceased before David's time and were apparently among the less faithful Israelites, it's impossible to second guess the era in which these several poems were penned.

The message here is deeper than it may at first appear. Compare the contents of **Psalm 45** to the **Song of Solomon,** which probably predates it even though this psalm appears first in our Bibles. In light of what we know about New Testament times, these lines certainly seem to be prophetic of the relationship of the Christ (the Hebrew word was *Messiah*) and His believers. That's worth a second reading!

PSALM 50

Psalm 50:16–18, 21–22. *But to the wicked God says . . . You hate discipline, and you cast my words behind you . . . You keep company with adulterers . . . These things you have done, and I have been silent; you thought that I was one like yourself. But now I rebuke you and lay the charge before you. Mark this, then, you who forget God, lest I tear you apart, and there be none to deliver!"*

One of several hymns penned by Asaph, this one gives some of the actions God classifies as *wicked,* including that they *keep company with adulterers.*

PSALM 51

Psalm 51:1–4. *Have mercy on me, O God, according to your steadfast love; according to your abundant mercy blot out my transgressions. Wash me thoroughly from my iniquity, and cleanse me from my sin! For I know my* *transgressions, and my sin is ever before me. Against you, you only, have I sinned and done what is evil in your sight, so that you may be justified in your words and blameless in your judgment.*

This psalm of David was penned after the prophet Nathan accused him of his adulterous actions with Bathsheba—and his arranged death of her husband, Uriah. Notice here, especially in the final sentence of that segment, that David's coveting, adultery, and murder were first and foremost sins against God.

Psalm 51:5. *Behold, I was brought forth in iniquity, and in sin did my mother conceive me.*

Does this mean David was conceived out of wedlock? That's doubtful since he was the youngest of several children. Therefore, this would refer to the original sin nature that humans inherit from Adam and Eve—now part of our DNA.

Psalm 51:6. *Behold, you delight in truth in the inward being, and you teach me wisdom in the secret heart.*

This, of course, is where David's sin with Bathsheba started—in that part of his being where emotions reside.

Psalm 51:7–17. *Purge me with hyssop, and I shall be clean; wash me, and I shall be whiter than snow. Let me hear joy and gladness; let the bones that you have broken rejoice. Hide your face from my sins, and blot out all my iniquities. Create in me a clean heart, O God, and renew a right spirit within me. Cast me not away from your presence, and take not your Holy Spirit from me. Restore to me the joy of your salvation, and uphold me with a willing spirit. Then I will teach transgressors your ways, and sinners will return to you. Deliver me from bloodguiltiness, O God, O God of my salvation, and my tongue will sing aloud of your righteousness. O Lord, open my lips, and my mouth will declare your praise. For you will not delight in sacrifice, or I would give it; you will not be pleased with a burnt offering. The sacrifices of God are a broken spirit; a broken and contrite heart, O God, you will not despise.*

There is hope because God forgives those who admit their wrong and trust His promises.

Psalm 51 thus relates back to **2 Samuel 11** and **12.** This is not an "Uh-oh, I got caught" reaction to the reprimand from God's messenger. Instead, it indicates that David was well aware of the wrong of all his thoughts and actions regarding Uriah and Bathsheba and was seriously repentant.

God didn't bring Uriah back to life, and the baby that was born of that adulterous union died shortly thereafter as one of the consequences of David's actions, but God did bless the marriage of King David and the now-widowed Bathsheba, forgave them both, and renewed the communication link by which the Holy Spirit continued to guide David's further actions and writings.

PSALM 106

Psalm 106:34–42. *They did not destroy the peoples, as the* LORD *commanded them, but they mixed with the nations and learned to do as they did. They served their idols, which became a snare to them. They sacrificed their sons and their daughters to the demons; they poured out innocent blood, the blood of their sons and daughters, whom they sacrificed to the idols of Canaan, and the land was polluted with blood. Thus they became unclean by their acts, and played the whore in their deeds. Then the anger of the* LORD *was kindled against his people, and he abhorred his heritage; he gave them into the hand of the nations, so that those who hated them ruled over them. Their enemies oppressed them, and they were brought into subjection under their power.*

This psalm includes a very long list of times in Hebrew history when God's people had *done wickedness,* beginning with the time of the **Exodus** and proceeding through at least **Judges,** in each case remembering how the Lord had rescued them. This section mentions mixed marriages, child sacrifice, and cult prostitution. No writer is cited.

PSALMS 113 AND 128

Psalm 113:9 and Psalm 128:1–3, both of whose authors are unknown, remind us that God is the one who allows children to be conceived in His timing and with the combination of genes that He has chosen for each particular child. When a childless couple finally is blessed with a baby, it is indeed an occasion to praise the Lord.

PSALM 127

Psalm 127:3–5 (NIrV). *Children are a gift from the* LORD. *They are a reward from him. Children who are born to people when they are young are like arrows in the hands of a soldier. Blessed are those who have many children. They won't be put to shame when they go up against their enemies in court.*"[38]

This is one of several psalms from the pen of Solomon. With 700 wives and 300 concubines, he must indeed have fathered a multitude of children.

PSALM 139

Psalm 139:13–16 (Beck). *You created my inner being and wove me together in my mother's womb. I thank You for how marvelously and wonderfully I am made . . . My limbs weren't hidden from You when I was made in secret and skillfully woven as in depths of the earth. Your eyes saw me before I was formed; before a single one of my days took shape they were all prepared and written in Your scroll.*

This psalm of David once more reinforces God's hand in the formation of a baby, from its very early stages of development. We are also reminded that each one is a person from the point of conception.

PROVERBS

Most of the verses in the remaining three books of Wisdom Literature come to us from the pen of Solomon—he who had 700 wives and 300 concubines. It's little surprise, therefore, that his writings would include a great deal concerning *God's Word about Sex*. These are still poetry, so those rules of structure would apply, but his thoughts aren't separated into individual songs. In order to make our exploring easier, I've grouped these verses by topic.

The logistics of Solomon's family blow me away. Imagine, a thousand women with only one husband!

Solomon had to be extremely rich in order to feed, clothe, and house that many dependents. Although they probably lived in dormitory settings, that's a large number to provide for. Apparently, he was exceedingly wealthy, plus, he could always use tax money to support his royal household.

A number of them would have had children as well—all of whom were sons and daughters of Solomon. The percentage of those sexual unions which would have resulted in pregnancies is anybody's guess. Were fertile women put back into the rotation? Were those who didn't become with child on first exposure given a second chance? Solomon was possibly twenty when he was crowned, and he ruled for forty years. Do the math.

Some of them—the concubines, for instance—may have been servants for the rest of the women. Given that those women were to be strictly for Solomon's benefit, they were probably at least a bit secluded from the rest of the population. How would you keep that many women and children busy enough to stay out of trouble?

Think of what that situation would do to the social balance of the rest of the community and nation as well as their neighbors. Many of those women were foreign imports. Since Solomon fought no battles, the surrounding kings and other leaders must have sent him several of their young ladies in an effort to appease him so he wouldn't follow in King David's footsteps. I suspect a number were also taken from the local population.

Thus, you had a thousand women, one husband (who is also the king), and a city with a significant number of young men who may well have felt they couldn't find a wife because the cream of the crop had already been taken. In spite of the attraction of being the king's wife, might some of those women have tried to turn to prostitution, especially since that had been a part of the religion they brought with them?

The admonitions of **Proverbs** are addressed to the writer's son. They are excellent advice for all boys and men in every generation. They might also have been written as a reminder to others in the community to leave King Solomon's women alone.

FORBIDDEN UNIONS

As we study these three sections, especially the book of **Proverbs,** keep in mind these points from Solomon's history:

Solomon was a son of King David and Bathsheba. His mother had been the wife of Uriah at the time David first had intercourse with her, thus, she was a *forbidden woman.* Solomon was well aware of the problems that relationship caused within David's household, in spite of the fact that David and Bathsheba were married shortly after Uriah was murdered.

A large number of Solomon's wives were foreigners or members of other nations who were still living inside the perimeters of the Promised Land. They were idol worshipers who eventually led Solomon to accept and fund (and perhaps fully embrace) their religions. Thus, they all also qualified as *forbidden women*. The influence those women had on Solomon was the reason God split the descendants of Jacob into two separate nations as soon as Solomon died.

Remember, also, that cult prostitution was included in the worship of those idols.

In light of all that, it's amazing how large a portion of **Proverbs** consists of warnings to avoid the *forbidden woman*, whether the neighbor's wife or the prostitute.

Proverbs 2:16–19 (Beck). *Wisdom will also save you from the strange woman, from the foreign woman with her smooth talk, who leaves the man she married when she was young and forgets the covenant with her God. Her house sinks down to death, and her ways lead you to the shades of death. None who have sexual intercourse with her come back or ever reach the paths of life.*

Proverbs 5:3–14. *For the lips of a forbidden woman drip honey, and her speech is smoother than oil, but in the end she is bitter as wormwood, sharp as a two-edged sword. Her feet go down to death . . . Keep your way far from her . . . lest you give your honor to others and your years to the merciless . . . and at the end of your life you groan, when your flesh and body are consumed, and you say, "How I hated discipline . . . I am at the brink of utter ruin."*

Proverbs 6:23–29. *The reproofs of discipline are the way of life, to preserve you from the evil woman, from the smooth tongue of the adulteress. Do not desire her beauty in your heart, and do not let her capture you with her eyelashes; for the price of a prostitute is only a loaf of bread, but a married woman hunts down a precious life . . . none who touches her will go unpunished.*

Proverbs 6:32–33. *He who commits adultery lacks sense; he who does it destroys himself. He will get wounds and dishonor, and his disgrace will not be wiped away.*

Proverbs 7:4–27. If you pray for wisdom and insight, they will *keep you from the forbidden woman, from the adulteress with her smooth words.*

Instead, those *lacking sense* will go looking for her.

The woman meets him, dressed as a prostitute, wily of heart. She is loud and wayward; her feet do not stay at home; now in the street, now in the market, and at every corner she lies in wait . . . "Come, let us take our fill of love till morning; let us delight ourselves with love. For my husband is not at home; he has gone on a long journey; he took a bag of money with him; at full moon he will come home." With much seductive speech she persuades him; with her smooth talk she compels him. All at once he follows her . . . As a bird rushes into a snare; he does not know that it will cost him his life . . . Do not stray into her paths, for many a victim has she laid low, and all her slain are a mighty throng . . . going down to the chambers of death.

Proverbs 9:13–18, 22:14, 23:27–28, 29:3, and **30:20** all reinforce the same thought.

Did you get the message? Ladies and gentlemen, stay far away from any facet of that activity. Sexually transmitted diseases are only the beginning of the problems that are involved.

MARRIAGE: POSITIVE VS. NEGATIVE

Proverbs 5:18–20. *Let your fountain be blessed, and rejoice in the wife of your youth, a lovely deer, a graceful doe. Let her breasts fill you at all times with delight; be intoxicated always in her love. Why should you be intoxicated, my son, with a forbidden woman and embrace the bosom of an adulteress?*

Proverbs 12:4. *An excellent wife is the crown of her husband, but she who brings shame is like rottenness in his bones.*

Proverbs 14:1. *The wisest of women builds her house, but folly with her own hands tears it down.*

Proverbs 15:17. *Better is a dinner of herbs where love is than a fattened ox and hatred with it.*

Proverbs 18:22. *He who finds a wife finds a good thing and obtains favor from the* LORD.

Proverbs 19:13–14. *A foolish son is ruin to his father, and a wife's quarreling is a continual dripping of rain. House and wealth are inherited from fathers, but a prudent wife is from the* LORD.

CONSTANT ARGUMENTS UPSET A HOUSEHOLD

Proverbs 17:1. *Better is a dry morsel with quiet than a house full of feasting with strife.*

Proverbs 21:9 and **25:24.** *It is better to live in a corner of the housetop than in a house shared with a quarrelsome wife.*

Proverbs 27:15–16 agrees, adding *to restrain her is to restrain the wind or to grasp oil in one's right hand.*

Proverbs 21:19 continues the same thought.

Imagine the amount of quarreling, in-fighting, and other dissension in each of Solomon's harems/dormitories, especially since those ladies were stuck with each other twenty-four/seven! It's no wonder Solomon occasionally wished for a quiet corner of a housetop. I'll bet the women weren't any happier with the arrangement than he was, in spite of the prestige it brought to their families that one of their own was a princess to the king.

ASSORTED MAXIMS FOR MARRIAGES AND FAMILIES

Proverbs 10:23 (Beck). *Doing something lewd is fun for a fool, but wisdom is the intelligent person's fun.*

Proverbs 11:22. *Like a gold ring in a pig's snout is a beautiful woman without discretion.*

Proverbs 11:29. *Whoever troubles his own household will inherit the wind.*

Proverbs 15:25. *The LORD tears down the house of the proud but maintains the widow's boundaries.*

Proverbs 17:6. *Grandchildren are the crown of the aged, and the glory of children is their fathers.*

Proverbs 17:13. *If anyone returns evil for good, evil will not depart from his house.*

Proverbs 25:28. *A man without self-control is like a city broken into and left without walls.*

Proverbs 30 and **31** did not come from the pen of Solomon. **Proverbs 30** was authored by *Agur son of Jakeh.* **Proverbs 31** was written by *King Lemuel,* but he credits his mother for teaching him this description of the ideal wife. While we know nothing more of Agur or Lemuel, some translations identify both as being from Massa, who was one of those listed in **Genesis 25** as a son of Ishmael (the son of Abraham and his concubine Hagar). That would lead us to believe these two writers may well have belonged to one of the nomadic Arabic tribes inhabiting the nations surrounding Israel.

Proverbs 30:15–16. *Three things are never satisfied; four never say, "Enough": Sheol, the barren womb, the land never satisfied with water, and the fire that never says, "Enough."*

Proverbs 30:18–19. *Three things are too wonderful for me; four I do not understand: the way of an eagle in the sky, the way of a serpent on a rock, the way of a ship on the high seas, and the way of a man with a virgin.*

Proverbs 30:21–23. *Under three things the earth trembles; under four it cannot bear up: a slave when he becomes king, and a fool when he is filled with food; an unloved woman when she gets a husband, and a maidservant when she displaces her mistress.*

We have only to look at the situation between Sarah and Hagar to verify that last phrase.

THE PERFECT WIFE

Proverbs 31:10–31. *An excellent wife who can find? She is far more precious than jewels. The heart of her husband trusts in her, and he will have no lack of gain. She does him good, and not harm, all the days of her life . . .*

She manufactures cloth, starting with fibers, making sheets, blankets, and clothing for her family and servants, then selling some of those products, working all night if necessary, but that's just the start.

She is like the ships of the merchant; she brings her food from afar. She rises while it is yet night and provides food for her household and portions for her maidens. She considers a field and buys it; with the fruit of her hands she plants a vineyard. She dresses herself with strength and makes her arms strong . . . She opens her hand to the poor and reaches out her hands to the needy . . . Her husband is known in the gates when he sits among the elders of the land . . . Strength and dignity are her clothing, and she laughs at the time to come. She opens her mouth with wisdom, and the teaching of kindness is on her tongue. She looks well to the ways of her household and does not eat the bread of idleness. Her children rise up and call her blessed; her husband also, and he praises her: "Many women have done excellently, but you surpass them all." Charm is deceitful, and beauty is vain, but a woman who fears the LORD is to be praised. Give her of the fruit of her hands, and let her works praise her in the gates.

She is Wonder Woman! Even with all our modern appliances, we will never measure up to this lady, though many of us would wish for all those talents.

ECCLESIASTES

Ecclesiastes 2:1–11 (Beck). *I said to myself I'll try pleasure and enjoy myself. But that also was a vapor. I said about laughter, it doesn't make any sense, and* *about pleasure, what does it accomplish? I tried to find out what happened when I stimulate my body with wine (my mind being wisely in control); and I also took hold of foolishness till I could see what is best for human beings to do under the sun during the short time of their life . . .*

Solomon lists a variety of things that should have brought enjoyment, including . . . *I enjoyed the pleasures men have with concubines . . . I didn't keep from my eyes anything they wanted or refuse to let my heart have any pleasure since my heart found pleasure in my work . . . But when I turned to look at everything I made and all the work I did, it was all a vapor, like trying to catch the wind, with nothing gained under the sun.*

Self-indulgence leads only to depression and despair.

Ecclesiastes 3:1–2. *For everything there is a season, and a time for every matter under heaven: a time to be born, and a time to die; a time to plant, and a time to pluck up what is planted.*

These lines were used by The Byrds in a very popular song from the "Dark Ages" when I was young. Notice that both birth and death happen in the Lord's timing, not by man's decision.

Ecclesiastes 3:5. *. . . a time to embrace, and a time to refrain from embracing;*

Ecclesiastes 3:8. *a time to love, and a time to hate; a time for war, and a time for peace.*

The Bible was probably the furthest thing from the minds of the teens who made that song popular, but that is indeed where Pete Seeger obtained the lyrics.

Ecclesiastes 6:3. *If a man fathers a hundred children and lives many years, so that the days of his years are many, but his soul is not satisfied with life's good things, and he also has no burial, I say that a stillborn child is better off than he.*

To have fathered one hundred children, the man must have had many wives at the same time. Note this also didn't bring happiness.

Ecclesiastes 7:26. *And I find something more bitter than death: the woman whose heart is snares and nets, and whose hands are fetters. He who pleases God escapes her, but the sinner is taken by her.*

That sounds a lot like several of the **Proverbs** warnings against the forbidden woman.

Ecclesiastes 9:9. *Enjoy life with the wife whom you love, all the days of your vain life that he has given you under the sun, because that is your portion in life and in your toil at which you toil under the sun.*

Think of the many long-time, happy marriages there were in past generations. Would that, someday, such will again be the norm rather than the exception.

SONG OF SONGS—BY SOLOMON

Modern English translations of the **Song of Solomon** have headings to indicate who is speaking. Thus, they read like a drama manuscript or a play. The King James translation didn't include those indicators because those words were actually not in the original Hebrew, but the pronouns have been determined from the verbs that were used, in addition to other internal clues. That this is possible shouldn't surprise anyone who has studied a foreign language, for many other tongues assign gender to all nouns and verbs, including inanimate objects, even though English-speaking Americans shake their heads and ask how a rose can be masculine in Spanish but feminine in German.

Of Solomon's 700 wives and 300 concubines, I think it most likely that the woman in this Hebrew poem was the queen of Sheba. She would have been dark **(1:5–6)**, and as a reigning monarch, she certainly would have caught Solomon's attention.

A majority of Christian theologians will say that this entire book is really a word picture of Christ and His faithful believers. Such is their emphasis on that theological interpretation that they tend to totally ignore the possibility that Solomon wrote these chapters as the account of a romance between two physical humans—a groom and a bride. While they do have spiritual significance, these chapters can also be taken at face value—the primary way these words were probably perceived for centuries. Therefore, at this point in our study, let's first consider **Song of Solomon** from a strictly human standpoint.

According to Lutheran theologian Reverend Doctor Chris Mitchell, author of *The Song of Songs*,[39] ". . . Church fathers refer to a tradition of Jewish rabbis who prohibited younger men (probably those who were under thirty years old, and who may not have been married), from reading the Song of Songs . . ." He cites St. Jerome, who lived from 347 to 420 AD, two other "early church Christian interpreters," and Martin Luther as having alluded to that practice in their writings.

If the Old Testament rabbis wouldn't allow any unmarried man under the age of thirty to read that scroll, this indicates to me that those spiritual leaders also, at least, saw the physical message in Solomon's words.

Whether you, the reader of this book, qualify under those age guidelines or not, it's time for you to do some research directly in God's Word. In all standard translations, if you ignore introductions, dictionaries, and concordances, **Psalms** will be in the middle of the book. **Song of Solomon** usually starts about fifty pages after that early hymnal ends. Read it once as a human romance, then again with a spiritual interpretation.

When you have done so, come back to this book, and we'll explore some of those passages.

WHAT DID YOU DISCOVER?

Welcome back to the conclusion of what the Bible says about sex in roughly the first half of God's Book. If you skipped my directions in the last two paragraphs, go back. Now. Find a Bible, either a paper and ink copy or one of the modern, digital versions. Bible Gateway (www.biblegateway.com) is an excellent website. There you can choose from fifty different English translations, or even read Scripture in a foreign language.

You need to become convinced that those words really are in the Bible. Many people will tell you that God is anti-sex. **Song of Solomon** declares that nothing could be further from the truth. These eight chapters are filled with allusions to a wedding, complete with thoughts and events leading up to the actual marriage and beyond. As a matter of fact, the details are quite graphic. I can easily understand why youngsters are not ready for those pages.

Now that you have read those chapters for yourself, which interpretation was the easiest to visualize? Was it the human/physical relationship between groom and bride? For many of us, that would certainly be the first idea that would come to mind.

In fact, looking from that viewpoint, perhaps you had some questions. I certainly did.

For instance, was Solomon right-handed or left-handed? Both **2:6** and **8:3** give us hints.

Song of Songs 6:8–9 (Beck) says, *There may be sixty queens, eighty concubines, and virgins without number, but my dove, my perfect one, is unique.* We know that Solomon had 700 wives and 300 concubines—eventually— so the queen of Sheba must have come to Jerusalem rather early in his reign. **1 Kings 11:4** (Beck) tells us *as Solomon grew old, his wives turned his heart away to follow other gods, and he was no more altogether true to the LORD his God, as his father David had been.*

Apparently, the majority of those thousand women were introduced to the palace after the lady who took center stage in this long poem had returned to her home. Thus, we might suspect that her visit was not in the waning days of Solomon's reign.

Given the details of **Song of Songs**, we also would not be surprised at the theories, discussed in chapter five, that suggest that the queen was pregnant when she returned to Sheba. That would, indeed, fit right into the picture.

Never let it be said that the Bible is dull.

Now, to look at **Song of Songs** through our theological glasses, we will definitely have to shift gears. The concept of God as groom and His people as His bride does take some getting used to. Lest we think the idea only hatched recently, God declared Himself to be *a jealous God* twice in **Exodus (20:5** and **34:14)** and at least three times in **Deuteronomy (4:24, 5:9,** and **6:15)**.

As I study the prophets in preparation of the companion volume to this book, they almost all compare their nations' relationship with God to that of a human husband and wife. In each case, the prophet's verdict is that the bride has been wantonly unfaithful, pursuing alternatives to the Lord *on every high hill and under every green tree* (**Jeremiah 2:20**).

The prophets are also much more graphic than **Song of Songs**. Thus, this husband/wife comparison definitely was not a new concept, hatched during a long summer in Babylon.

There are some interesting ties between this short book and the New Testament. For instance, the action described in **Song of Songs 5:2,** *My beloved is knocking,* is claimed by Jesus Himself in **Revelation 3:20,** *"Behold, I stand at the door and knock."*

Much more direct is the statement of John the Baptist, when instructing his own followers concerning the identity of Jesus. In **John 3:28–29,** John tells his disciples, *"You yourselves bear me witness, that I said, 'I am not the Christ, but I have been sent before him.' The one who has the bride is the bridegroom. The friend of the bridegroom, who stands and hears him, rejoices greatly at the bridegroom's voice. Therefore this joy of mine is now complete."* Basically, that ties the entire book of **Song of Solomon** to Jesus.

The really mind-boggling concept here is the idea that Jesus, God the Son, apparently finds *us* attractive. That would certainly be the message concerning Bridegroom and bride in **Song of Songs**. He knows every inch of our bodies—the cancer cells we haven't discovered yet, the damages we've inflicted by our lifestyles, as well as every thought that has ever marched through our minds, including the hate, fear, jealousy, greed, and rebellion—and in spite of it all, He loves us. We don't even like ourselves sometimes, but He loves us. He even died for us. Just like many an earthly groom, He has built a new home for us. He promises to come back to get us and take us there.

Thank You, Lord. We look forward to Your arrival. Meanwhile, for the time we remain on this earth, help us to pay better attention to Your Word and to apply it to our lives.

LOOKING FORWARD

What did the prophets have to say about the mess God's people had allowed themselves to be in? What were Jesus' views on sex? Are we still expected to adhere to the rules of the Old Testament? Do the epistles add new regulations?

These interesting questions are still waiting to be answered. I will attempt to shed light on those issues when we reconvene our exploration of *God's Word about Sex* in Book Two, beginning with the prophecy of **Isaiah.**

THANKS

MANY HAVE BEEN most helpful in bringing this book from idea to print. I especially want to thank the following:

LC-MS Pastor Gerhard Grabenhofer, who provided definitions of occasional Greek and Hebrew words, then did a theological review of the entire manuscript. Much tweaking has happened since his examination, but the document, as he last saw it, passed inspection.

Dr. Chris Mitchell of Concordia Publishing House, who graciously shared with me some of his work on **Song of Solomon**.

Aletha, Caroline, Deanna, Deb, Deb, Gail, Juli, Laurie, Liz, Mary, Nickie, Rita, Susie, Tammy, and other readers who shared their comments with me concerning portions of this book.

Friends and family members who provided transportation when I couldn't drive.

The Wordsowers Christian Writers group in Omaha, from whom I have learned so much.

The wonderful people of Electric Moon Publishing, who have turned a manuscript into a book.

Most important of all, thank You, Lord, for letting me participate in this project of bringing Your words to those who have read *God's Word about Sex.*

—**Mary Kuhlmann Antholz**

ABOUT THE AUTHOR

MARY KUHLMANN ANTHOLZ grew up on a farm in the middle of Nebraska. She has been single, married, divorced, a single mom, a mother-in-law, and now a grandmother.

Following the example of her first college roommate, at seventeen Mary started reading the Bible daily. Cover to cover and back to the beginning, it's a habit she has now enjoyed for almost sixty years.

NOTES

1. H. C. Leupold, *Exposition of Genesis,* Volume 1 (Grand Rapids, Michigan: Baker Book House, twenty-sixth printing, 1992); (The Wartburg Press, Copyright 1942, 171–172).

2. For more about the Hebrew word *toledoth,* see Henry M. Morris, *The Genesis Record* (Grand Rapids, Michigan: Baker Books, 1976), 25–30.

3. John D. Morris, Ph.D., "Have Sodom and Gomorrah Been Discovered?" www.icr.org/article/have-sodom-gomorrah-been-discovered.

4. Henry M. Morris III, *The Book of Beginnings, Volume 3,* (Dallas, Texas: Institute for Creation Research, 2014), 96. ". . . The physical gesture is that the one making the promise is to place his hand under the other's genitals, thus symbolically embracing the entire family line in his promise."

5. www.britannica.com/topic/Hittite characterizes the Hittite religion as "tolerant polytheism." Their king "was not only the chief ruler, military leader, and supreme judge but also the earthly deputy of the storm god; upon dying, he himself became a god."

6. www.eastonsbibledictionary.org/2401-Mandrakes.php.

7. H. C. Leupold, *Exposition of Genesis,* Volume 2 (Grand Rapids, Michigan: Baker Book House, thirteenth printing, 1975), 1001.

8. According to R. Laird Harris, Gleason L. Archer Jr., and Bruce K. Waltke, *Theological Wordbook of the Old Testament, Volume 2,* (Chicago: Moody Press, 1980), the Hebrew word *Sheol* is variously translated as grave, hell, or pit. They say, "The KJV uses 'grave' thirty-one times, 'hell' thirty times, 'pit' three times." Many other versions, like the ESV, apparently don't even translate the term but simply print it as *Sheol.*

9. See copyright citation in Foreword.

10. www.britannica.com/topic/adultery.

11. www.gotquestions.org/who-Molech.html describes the idols as "giant metal statues of a man with a bull's head. Each image had a hole in the abdomen and possibly outstretched forearms that made a kind of ramp to the hole. A fire was lit in or around the statue. Babies were placed in the statue's arms or in the hole." In addition, https://biblehub.com/topical/m/molech.htm quotes *Smith's Bible Dictionary*, "According to Jewish tradition, the image of Molech was of brass, hollow within, and was situated without Jerusalem. 'His face was (that) of a calf, and his hands stretched forth like a man who opens his hands to receive (something) of his neighbor. And they kindled it with fire, and the priests took the babe and put it into the hands of Molech, and the babe gave up the ghost.'"

12. *"God hates divorce"* is not the only way this verse in Malachi can be translated. Bible Gateway shows twenty-five translations using first person (*God says, "I hate divorce"*), six with the same idea but in third person, eight use *"putting away"* instead of *"divorce"*—but the remaining twelve speak instead of a man hating his wife, which is a totally different concept.

13. See www.biblegateway.com/verse/en/Matthew%205:32 for most English translations of Matthew 5:32.

14. F. Hauck and S. Schulz, as found in pages 918–921 of *Theological Dictionary of the New Testament: Abridged* in one volume by Geoffrey W. Bromiley, (Wm. B Eerdmans Publishing Co., Grand Rapids, Michigan, 1985).

15. Gerrit Verkuyl Ph.D., editor, *The Holy Bible – The New Berkeley Version in Modern English*, (Grand Rapids, Michigan: Zondervan Publishing House, 1969), 254.

16. **Judges 3:11, 30; 5:31; 8:28.**

17. www.britannica.com/topic/concubinage

18. www.eastonsbibledictionary.org/875–Concubine.php.

19. Creation.com/images/pdfs/other/timeline_of_the_bible.pdf estimates that **Ruth** lived around 1100 BC

20. In fact, www.merriam-webster.com/dictionary/camp%20followers gives as its first definition "CAMP FOLLOWER: a civilian (such as a prostitute) who follows a military unit to attend or exploit military personnel."

21. Rizpah shows up again in **2 Samuel 21:10–14,** where she kept predators away from the bodies of her two sons when David handed them over to the Gibeonites, who hung them in retaliation for King Saul's actions against the people of that community.

22. Probably Amman, the present capital of Jordan, according to www.merriam-webster.com/dictionary/Rabbah%20Ammon.

23. See Joseph's reaction to Potiphar's wife in **Genesis 39:9.**

24. Geshur was possibly an area in Syria between Mount Hermon and the Sea of Galilee, according to *Easton's Bible Dictionary,* www.eastonsbibledictionary.org/1469-Geshur.php.

25. www.biblicalarchaeology.org/daily/ancient-cultures/ancient-near-eastern-world/who-is-the-queen-of-sheba-in-the-bible; Dr. Paul L. Maier's book (as a translator) *Josephus: The Essential Works* (Grand Rapids, Michigan, Kregel Publications, 1988, 1994) indicates she was "queen of Egypt and Ethiopia." Apparently, that ancient historian did not mention the supposed descendants of her visit with Solomon.

26. www.britannica.com/biography/Queen-of-Sheba.

27. See quotation from *The Holy Bible – The New Berkeley Version in Modern English*, found in chapter two in my comments on **Numbers 25:2–5.**

28. www.gotquestions.net/Printer/Molech-PF.html.

29. www.eastonsbibledictionary.org/785-Chemosh.php.

30. www.merriam-webster.com/dictionary/Jezebel.

31. www.biblegateway.com/verse/en/2%20Kings%208:16.

32. *Lexham English Bible* (LEB) 2012 by Logos Bible Software. Lexham is a registered trademark of Logos Bible Software and New American Bible (Revised Edition) (NABRE).

33. Between northeast Palestine and the Euphrates, as per www.eastonsbible-dictionary.org/280-Aram.php.

34. See River Gozan article and maps, bibleatlas.org/regional/gozan.htm; *Easton's Bible Dictionary* says it's "on the river Habor . . . a tributary of the Euphrates," www.eastonsbibledictionary.org/1537-Gozan.php.

35. Apparently east or southeast of the Dead Sea, www.eastonsbibledictionary.org/3262-Seir.php.

36. www.merriam-webster.com/dictionary/xerxes.

37. www.britannica.com/topic/eunuch, www.merriam-webster.com/dictionary/eunuch.

38. This Scripture is taken from the *Holy Bible, NEW INTERNATIONAL READER'S VERSION®.* Copyright © 1996, 1998 Biblica.

39. *Concordia Commentary: The Song of Songs,* (St. Louis: Concordia Publishing House, 2003).

Electric Moon Publishing, LLC is a custom, independent publisher who assists indie authors, ministries, businesses, and organizations with their book publishing needs. Services include writing, editing, design, layout, print, e-book, marketing, and distribution. For more information please use the contact form found on www.emoonpublishing.com.

Made in the USA
Monee, IL
09 October 2020

44381078R10108